United Arab Emirates

United Arab Emirates

BY LIZ SONNEBORN

Enchantment of the World™
Second Series

Children's Press®

An Imprint of Scholastic Inc.

NEW YORK TORONTO LONDON AUCKLAND SYDNEY
MEXICO CITY NEW DELHI HONG KONG
DANBURY, CONNECTICUT

Frontispiece: The marina in Dubai

Consultant: Peter Sluglett, Professor of Middle Eastern History, University of Utah, Salt Lake City

Please note: All statistics are as up-to-date as possible at the time of publication.

Book production by Herman Adler

Library of Congress Cataloging-in-Publication Data

Sonneborn, Liz.
  United Arab Emirates / by Liz Sonneborn.
    p. cm.—(Enchantment of the world. Second series)
  Includes bibliographical references and index.
  ISBN-13: 978-0-531-18487-5
  ISBN-10: 0-531-18487-0
  1. United Arab Emirates—Juvenile literature. I. Title.
  DS247.T8S66 2008
  953.57—dc22 SON.   2007019641

© 2008 by Liz Sonneborn.
All rights reserved. Published in 2008 by Children's Press, an imprint of Scholastic Inc.
Published simultaneously in Canada.
Printed in the United States of America.   44

SCHOLASTIC, CHILDREN'S PRESS, and associated logos are trademarks and/or registered trademarks of Scholastic Inc.
1 2 3 4 5 6 7 8 9 10 R 17 16 15 14 13 12 11 10 09 08

United Arab Emirates

Contents

Cover photo:
An Emirati resort

Liwa Oasis

Emirati food

Then and Now

8

IMAGINE A SEASIDE TOWN WHERE PEOPLE LIVE MUCH AS their ancestors did centuries ago. For most people in the town, it is a hand-to-mouth existence. They have little but the fruits of the sea. Once, men could make a decent living by diving into the waters and finding pearls on the seafloor, which they could trade for other goods. But now, there are few buyers for these precious objects, and people rely on fishing to make ends meet. Using traps woven from palm fronds, fishers work long hours to catch enough to feed their families. On a good day, they might have some left over to sell.

Opposite: **Fishermen pull in their nets in Abu Dhabi.**

Some Emiratis still fish on traditional wooden boats called dhows.

The work is exhausting. Outside, the air is thick with moisture and baked by an unrelenting sun. With temperatures rising as high as 120 degrees Fahrenheit (49 degrees Celsius), there is no escape from the blistering heat. Few people in the town have ever heard of air-conditioning. In fact, modern conveniences are virtually unknown. Their small homes have no electricity, no plumbing, not even running water.

There are no paved roads. Nor are there any telephones, radios, or televisions that could connect the people with the outside world. They may see a book or newspaper from time to time. But with no schools to teach them how to read and write, the words on the pages hold no meaning.

In the past, buildings in the United Arab Emirates were made of rock or mud bricks. Today, they are made of glass and steel.

Skyscrapers surround the marina in Dubai.

Into the Future

Next, imagine climbing into a time machine geared up to transport you to the same seaside town, but in the future. When you arrive, you can hardly believe you're in the place where that sleepy village once stood. Everything has been transformed. Along the beach are miles and miles of skyscrapers, their steel and glass gleaming in the hot sun. In the ocean, the old wooden fishing vessels are gone. The waters are crowded with enormous ships from around the globe.

As you look around, you see that the small town with unpaved roads has been replaced with a bustling city crisscrossed by highways clogged with luxury cars. And the people! The city is home to more than one million, and the population is growing quickly. Every year, five million visitors come to the city. Its streets are full of citizens from different countries. Some are speaking Arabic, others are speaking English, and still others are conversing in a host of other languages. It is easy to see that this is a modern city with international appeal.

Millions of people visit the UAE every year. Some come to enjoy the warm water, while others make business deals.

It is also clear that there is something for everyone here. Swimmers and sunbathers flock to the waterfront. Tourists sample the world-class restaurants and nightspots. Vacationers enjoy huge theme parks and major sporting events at brand-new arenas. Shoppers hurry off to the city's gigantic shopping malls. Businesspeople rush to the glittering office towers, eager to wheel and deal. In the office towers and on the streets, people are buying and selling. An astounding amount of money is changing hands. You hear that diamond-encrusted cell phones are one of the fastest-selling fashion accessories.

A Dynamic Nation

How far into the future did you travel in your time machine? Just how long did it take for the poor fishing town to turn into a spectacular metropolis? It was not thousands of years, or even hundreds. It was only about fifty years, from the middle of the twentieth century to the beginning of the twenty-first. The greatest changes have occurred since the 1980s.

The poor village that ballooned into a bustling city is a real place. It is Dubai, the largest city in the United Arab Emirates (UAE). The UAE is a small country in the Middle East, the part of Asia closest to Africa. Although the city of Dubai offers the most startling examples, just about everything in the UAE has been transformed in recent decades. The story of this exciting nation is all about change—how it has changed in the past and how it is likely to change in the future.

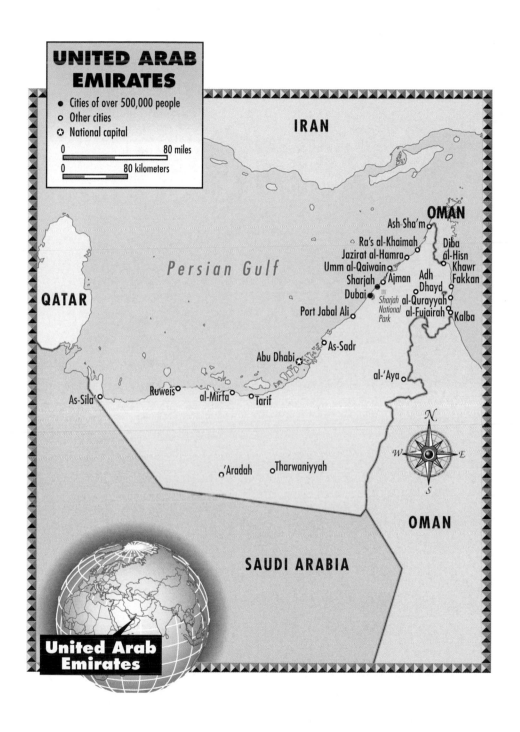

UNITED ARAB EMIRATES

- ● Cities of over 500,000 people
- ○ Other cities
- ✪ National capital

0   80 miles

0   80 kilometers

IRAN

OMAN

Ash Sha'm

Ra's al-Khaimah

Diba al-Hisn

Jazirat al-Hamra

Umm al-Qaiwain

Khawr Fakkan

Persian Gulf

Sharjah

Ajman

Adh Dhayd

Dubai

Sharjah National Park

al-Qurayyah

QATAR

Port Jabal Ali

al-Fujairah

Kalba

As-Sadr

Abu Dhabi

al-'Aya

As-Sila

Ruweis

al-Mirfa

Tarif

N

W   E

S

'Aradah

Tharwaniyyah

OMAN

United Arab Emirates

SAUDI ARABIA

A Varied Land

THE ARABIAN PENINSULA, SOMETIMES SIMPLY CALLED Arabia, is located in southwest Asia. This peninsula is home to eight nations, including the United Arab Emirates (UAE). Covering about 32,280 square miles (83,600 square kilometers), the UAE is a little smaller than the state of Maine. It stretches in a crescent shape across southeastern Arabia.

In addition to its mainland, the UAE controls two hundred islands. Among them is Das, which serves as a major site for oil operations. The UAE also claims the Tunb Islands and Abu Musa Island, although they are now occupied by Iran, the UAE's neighbor across the Persian Gulf.

Opposite: **The United Arab Emirates is a mixture of rippled sand dunes and rocky mountains.**

Futaisi Island is near Abu Dhabi. It is the site of ancient wells and an old mosque as well as a top country club.

The UAE is made up of seven small, independent states called emirates. Six of the seven emirates—Abu Dhabi, Dubai, Sharjah, Ajman, Umm al-Qaiwain, and Ra's al-Khaimah—lie along the southern shore of the Persian Gulf. The other emirate, al-Fujairah, also has a coastline. Its eastern border is the western coast of the Gulf of Oman in the Arabian Sea.

The UAE shares land borders with two other nations. Saudi Arabia lies to the south and west, and Oman lies to the north and east. The UAE's boundary with Saudi Arabia was set by treaties signed in the 1970s. But in many areas, the precise boundary between the two countries remains uncertain.

Making New Land

In 2001, Nakheel Properties began an ambitious construction project off the coast of Dubai City. Using sand dug up from the bottom of the Persian Gulf, the company is creating three enormous artificial land masses—the Palm Jumeirah, the Palm Jabal Ali, and the Palm Deira. Although they are called the Palm Islands, they are actually peninsulas because they are connected to the mainland. Each is designed to look like a palm tree with a crescent shape on top. They will eventually be covered with luxury hotels and apartments, restaurants, shopping malls, and theme parks. The biggest attraction, though, will be their beautiful beaches, which will stretch more than 320 miles (515 km).

Nakheel has an even bigger project in the works, appropriately called "the World." This will consist of three hundred artificial islands off Dubai, which together will form a gigantic map of the world. Some of the richest people on the planet are snatching up their own piece of the World. The islands are for sale at an average price of US$25 million each.

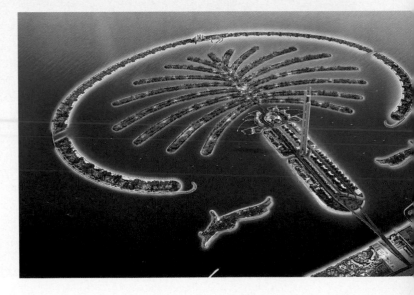

Abu Dhabi is by far the largest of the emirates, covering about four-fifths of the country. Most of Abu Dhabi's people are concentrated in its biggest city, also called Abu Dhabi. The capital of the UAE, Abu Dhabi City, rests on a T-shaped island just off the coast. Two bridges allow people to travel easily between Abu Dhabi and the mainland.

Abu Dhabi enjoys bright sunny skies throughout most of the year.

The Coastal Region

Most Emirati people live in Abu Dhabi or in other cities along the country's coastal plains. These urban centers include Sharjah, Ajman, and Dubai, the biggest city in the UAE. The coast is also home to the UAE's largest harbors—Port Rashid and Port Jabal Ali, near Dubai. Both of these ports are human-made. UAE harbors along the Gulf of Oman include Diba al-Hisn, Khawr Fakkan, and Kalba.

Emirati Enclaves

A small area named Madha is located within the emirate of Sharjah, but it is officially part of the country of Oman. Madha is an enclave—an area owned by one country that is completely surrounded by another.

Madha is not the only enclave in Sharjah. In the center of Madha is Nahwa, a tiny community of about forty houses that is part of the United Arab Emirates. Nahwa is one of the few enclaves-within-an-enclave anywhere in the world.

The UAE's Geographic Features

Highest Elevation: 5,010 feet (1,527 m), at Jabal Yibir

Lowest Elevation: Sea level along the coast

Largest Emirate: Abu Dhabi, 26,000 square miles (67,340 sq km)

Smallest Emirate: Ajman, 100 square miles (260 sq km)

Longest Border: With Saudi Arabia, 284 miles (457 km)

Hottest Month: July, average high temperature of 106°F (41°C)

Coolest Month: January, average high temperature of 75°F (24°C)

Driest Emirate: Abu Dhabi, average annual rainfall of 3 inches (7 cm)

Wettest Emirate: Sharjah, average annual rainfall of 19 inches (48 cm)

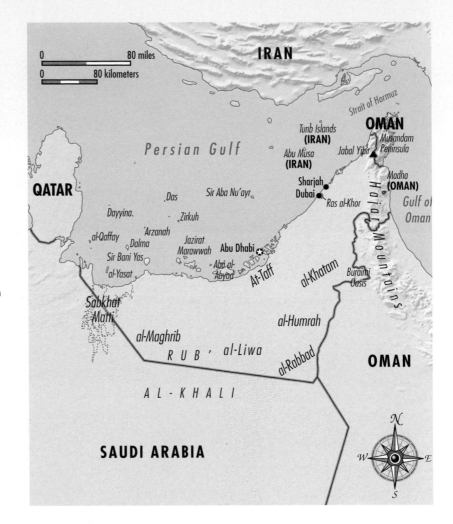

The land along the coast is largely flat. Heavy northern winds sometimes blow over the region, especially in the early summer. The winds carry sand and silt, creating dangerous dust storms. These storms darken the air, so that people can barely see anything in front of them.

The Desert Lands

South of the coast, the heavy winds blow strongly in one direction, creating sand dunes called barchans. Beautiful yet forbidding, these dunes form giant arcs of sand.

In the south and west of Abu Dhabi Emirate, the vast dunes merge into the great Arabian Desert. The desert is called the Rub al-Khali, or the Empty Quarter. There is little water, so as the name suggests, few people live there.

It's easy to get lost in the sand dunes in the UAE.

Some parts of the desert have enough underground water to sustain permanent settlements. These places are called oases. The country's largest oasis is al-Ain. It is the Emirati half of the Buraimi Oasis, which straddles the UAE–Oman border. Farther south, near the Saudi Arabian border, are a string of smaller oases called the Liwa. These oases are among the few areas in the UAE that can be farmed without irrigation.

On the western edge of the UAE's desert lands, along the border with Saudi Arabia, is the Sabkhat Matti, a huge salt flat. This region was once subject to frequent flooding. The salt left behind when the seawater evaporated created a crunchy crust on the surface of the land. Another, smaller salt flat lies southwest of Abu Dhabi City.

The Mountainous East

The UAE's coastal and desert lands are relatively low and flat. Far to the east, the landscape is very different. There, the land rises, reaching its highest point in the Hajar Mountains. This mountain range includes the UAE's tallest peak, Jabal Yibir, which rises to 5,010 feet (1,527 meters).

The ruins of a fortress sit high in the mountains outside al-Fujairah.

The Climate

The Hajar Mountains are the wettest part of the UAE. Some places in the mountains average 19 inches (48 centimeters) of rain per year. The coast gets less rain, averaging between 4 and 8 inches (10 and 20 cm) annually.

The UAE has no permanent rivers or lakes. But in the mountains, rainwater collects in valleys called wadis to create temporary rivers. The rainy season, which comes during winter, features short, intense downpours.

The UAE enjoys fairly temperate weather in the winter. The coolest month is January, when the average high temperature is 75°F (24°C). The mountainous region to the east is often cooler.

For much of the rest of the year, the UAE is extremely warm. The hottest month is July. At this time, the average high temperature is 106°F (41°C), but it often rises above 120°F (49°C). Air-conditioning is a modern convenience that is treasured by Emiratis today.

After a rain, water collects in wadis, riverbeds that are normally dry. This allows plants to grow there.

A Look at the UAE's Cities

With a population topping one million, Dubai (below) is the largest city in the UAE. Less than 20 percent of its residents are citizens of the UAE. The rest are foreigners who came to Dubai to work. The booming city offers plenty of jobs in the manufacturing, construction, and service industries. It has also established a variety of special tax-free zones, prompting companies from around the world to open factories and offices there.

In recent years, Dubai has also emerged as a playground for tourists. More than five million people visit each year. The city is filled with hotels, restaurants, and nightclubs, with more under construction each year. Dubai's beautiful Persian Gulf beaches are one of its main attractions. In the summer, the weather can be stifling hot, with average July temperatures rising to 105°F (41°C). But in the winter, with average January temperatures of 75°F (24°C), the city attracts tourists from across Europe and Asia, ready to swim in the Gulf waters and soak in the warming sun. Shopping also

lures tourists to Dubai. In its large outdoor markets, shoppers can find just about anything—from spices and carpets to luxurious gold jewelry and precious gems. Dubai also features many upscale shopping malls, including the largest mall in the Middle East.

The UAE's third-largest city, Sharjah (above), is home to half a million people. It is also a popular tourist destination. Sharjah stands in stark contrast to Dubai. Instead of being glitzy, it has established itself as the cultural center of the UAE. It is full of museums, theaters, and galleries that celebrate both modern art and the UAE's cultural traditions. Sharjah is also home to University City, a vast campus that includes the University of Sharjah and the Sharjah Library and features beautiful fountains and gardens.

Desert Life

WITH MOST OF THE UAE COVERED BY DESERT, YOU might expect that the country has little native plant and animal life. But in fact, the UAE has a wide variety of both. Its islands, coasts, and mountains are full of life. And even the forbidding desert has its share of hardy living things.

In the Desert

In the Liwa and al-Ain oases, Emiratis use irrigation to make the desert bloom. These areas are home to large stands of date

Farmers raise tomatoes, potatoes, and grass for animal feed in the Liwa Oasis.

palms, trees that produce sweet fruit much loved by Emiratis. In the rest of the desert, the land is so dry that only a few types of grasses and shrubs can survive. Many of these plants have deep roots, which allow them to tap into sources of water far underground.

The animals of the UAE's desert are far more common and varied than the native plant population. But all life in the desert, whether plant or animal, must have the ability to survive extreme heat.

The most common desert animals are reptiles. The UAE is home to more than fifty kinds of reptiles. Most are lizards and snakes. The lizards range in size from tiny geckos just a few inches long to lumbering monitor lizards, which can grow to more than 4 feet (1.2 m) long. Snake species include the horned viper and the sand boa. These snakes prey on insects, small lizards, and rodents. The moisture in the bodies of their victims gives the snakes the water they need to survive.

The desert is home to many types of insects, including flies and bees. Spiders and scorpions are also common. Scorpions can sometimes be seen scurrying over the sand. The hard exterior of their bodies holds in moisture, making them comfortable even on the hottest days.

The desert monitor burrows under the sand during the heat of day. When it emerges, it hunts snakes, lizards, birds, and any other creature it can find.

Several types of birds are native to the UAE's desert lands, including the hoopoe lark and the cream-colored courser. When the weather heats up in summer, these birds migrate to cooler areas. They return in winter, often joined by other migrating birds, including the houbara bustard.

The shy houbara bustard lives in arid regions. It feeds on seeds, insects, and other small creatures.

The desert is filled with small mammals, including hares, mice, and gerbils. These creatures are nocturnal, coming out of their burrows only at night, after the sun has gone down and the temperature has dropped. Some spend most of the hot summer burrowed under the sand.

Relocating Leptien's Lizard

In 2000, a new species of lizard was discovered in the UAE. Named Leptien's spiny-tailed lizard, this animal is only found in the Emirates.

Five years later, the UAE government discovered a large colony of Leptien's lizards in Abu Dhabi. Unfortunately, they were living by the city's international airport. Plans were in the works to build a new runway right through the area where the lizards lived.

So, before the runway was built, a new project began—catching the lizards and sending them to a new home. Several scientists and a large group of volunteers first had to figure out how to lure the animals into traps. They discovered that small pieces of watermelon and carrots did the trick. Using these tasty lures, they captured two hundred lizards. The creatures were released in an area where other Leptien's lizards live. Abu Dhabi plans to bring the lizards back after it constructs a protected area by the airport where they can thrive.

The Arabian Oryx

The Arabian oryx is a large antelope. It once lived across the Arabian Peninsula, wherever there was grass nearby. But in 1972, it became extinct in the wild. In recent years, herds of oryx have been reintroduced in Arabia, and several hundred of the beasts now run free. The oryx may have inspired the legend of the unicorn. When the oryx is viewed in profile, its two horns line up, making them appear to be just one horn.

Larger desert-dwelling animals, such as the Arabian oryx, used to be common in the UAE. But in recent decades, over-hunting has driven them close to extinction. The few larger mammals still living in the UAE include several types of gazelles and the small Rueppell's fox.

The animal most closely associated with the Arabian Desert is the camel. Camels have played a unique role in the traditional way of life in the UAE. Nomadic desert people, who once moved from place to place in search of water, used camels to carry their supplies. Camels also provided desert tribes with milk, wool, meat, and hides.

The camel is well adapted to the desert. Its flat feet keep it from sinking into the sand (similar to how snowshoes work), and its long lashes protect its eyes from blowing sand. Camels can eat tough desert plants, and they can drink enough water at one time to keep them alive for weeks without another drop.

Camels are sometimes 11 feet (3.4 m) long and stand 7.5 feet (2.3 m) at the shoulder.

Laughing doves are common in the parts of the UAE where water is available. They earned their name because their call sounds like a person laughing.

For bird-watchers, the most exciting place in the UAE is the coastal region. Mangrove trees, which are unusual because they can grow in saltwater marshes, provide a shady habitat for many different species. All year, the coastal areas are filled with birds such as palm doves and house sparrows.

The Peregrine Falcon

The national bird of the UAE is the peregrine falcon. The falcon is important in traditional Emirati culture. For centuries, Emiratis of the desert relied on falcons to obtain food during the winter. They did not eat these precious birds. Instead, they trapped falcons and then trained them to hunt houbara bustards, hares, or even gazelles.

Training a falcon is a difficult process. The falcon handler has to earn the trust of the animal. Today, Emirati men are still famous for falconry, though it is now a sport rather than a way of getting food.

In the spring and fall, the bird population shoots up a whopping 500 percent. During those seasons, many thousands of migrating birds take a rest stop along the Emirati coastline. Many migratory birds come to Ras al-Khor, a wetland reserve in Dubai. One of the few protected wildlife reserves in the middle of an urban area, it is famous for its colorful flamingos.

Every year, tourists, mainly from Europe, come to the UAE to get a look at the migrating birds. Bird-watchers especially enjoy seeing huge flocks of black Socotra cormorants diving into the ocean in search of fish.

Green turtles have large, paddle-shaped flippers that help them swim. They sometimes migrate more than 1,500 miles (2,500 km) between where they are born and their feeding grounds.

The UAE is home to rare sea life. Its coasts are feeding and nesting areas for green turtles, whales, and dolphins. A large population of dugongs, or sea cows, live near the islands.

Scuba divers are drawn to the magnificent coral reefs in the shallow waters off the coast. These underwater formations are made from the skeletons of tiny creatures called coral polyps. Colorful, living polyps attach themselves to the older, rocky layer. Coral reefs provide shelter for fish and other small marine animals.

In recent years, rising water temperatures, oil spills, and the development of the coastal areas have damaged the reefs. To help preserve the UAE's reefs, marine reserves have been established off the coast. In these areas, fishing is not allowed and boating is regulated. This helps protect the reefs and the creatures that live nearby.

In the Mountains

Much of the mountainous region has too little soil for many plants to grow. But along the wadis, lush green grasses and ferns flourish. The mountains attract a number of birds, ranging from the tiny black-and-white Hume's wheater to the lappet-faced vulture. Sometimes, people spot an eagle flying overhead. Five species of eagles live in the UAE.

The Hajar Mountains once teemed with majestic animals. But hunting has taken its toll on many species. Some, including the Arabian wolf and the striped hyena, no longer live in the UAE. Others have dangerously low populations.

One of the most spectacular mountain animals still living in the UAE is the Arabian leopard. Smaller than most leopard species, the Arabian leopard preys on the delicate but speedy Arabian mountain gazelle. When gazelles cannot be found, the leopard relies on birds, foxes, and goats for food.

The UAE is also home to the Arabian tahr, which is closely related to the wild goat. After 1982, the tahr was thought to have

The Arabian leopard is critically endangered. It is estimated that only about one hundred Arabian leopards live on the entire Arabian Peninsula.

disappeared from the UAE. But in 1995, a female tahr and her offspring were spotted at a watering hole. The sighting confirmed that this animal still survives in the UAE mountains.

The caracal lynx dwells in the northern emirates. It lives mostly in mountainous areas, where it can more easily hide from hunters. Strong and slender, the caracal has a light brown coat with distinctive black tufts of fur sticking up from its tall ears.

Caracals are nocturnal. They come out at night to hunt birds, rodents, and small antelope.

Sheikh Zayd established a nature reserve on Sir Bani Yas Island in 1971. It now has thriving populations of endangered creatures such as sand gazelles.

Preserving Wildlife

The growing number of extinct and endangered species has attracted the attention of the UAE's government. In fact, preserving the country's wildlife was a cause of special importance to Sheikh Zayd bin Sultan al-Nahayan, the president of the UAE from 1971 to 2004.

During his rule, the Dubai Wildlife Research Centre was founded. This organization studies plant and animal habitats and establishes wildlife preserves and zoos where endangered animals can be bred. Its efforts to protect the houbara bustard have been particularly successful. Sheikh Zayd also endorsed programs to plant gardens and establish parks, ensuring that the urban residents of the UAE would have access to green spaces.

Under Sheikh Zayd's leadership, the national government created the Federal Environmental Agency in 1993. This

Fishing is banned in some of the UAE's coastal waters. This helps keep fish populations healthy.

agency proposes laws encouraging wildlife conservation. It also encourages the seven emirates to cooperate in establishing and enforcing environmental policy for the whole nation.

The UAE has since adopted many laws to protect endangered animals. In Abu Dhabi, hunting of most animals has long been banned. In al-Fujairah, killing wildcats, including leopards and lynx, is now illegal. Along the coast, it is illegal to catch sea turtles or to take their eggs.

For some Emiratis, these laws have caused substantial hardship. Fishers, for instance, face stiff fines if they capture turtles in their traps. The desert tribes of Abu Dhabi rely on hunting for their food, so the hunting bans place their very survival in question. And shepherds who herd in the mountains resent their inability to kill the wildcats that stalk their flocks of sheep. As a result, the government has not just focused on preserving the nation's precious wildlife habitats. It also works to educate the public about the importance of making sacrifices now to protect the nation's environment for generations to come.

The Sharjah Desert Park

Outside of Sharjah City, people can learn about the plants and animals of the UAE at the Sharjah Natural History Museum and Desert Park. This park features exhibits on desert life. It also houses the Arabian Wildlife Center, where visitors can observe animals from everywhere in the Arabian Peninsula. More than a hundred types of wildflowers have been planted in the park's botanical garden. The park also includes a breeding program for endangered animals such as the Arabian leopard. The goal is to one day have enough healthy leopards to start reintroducing them into the wild.

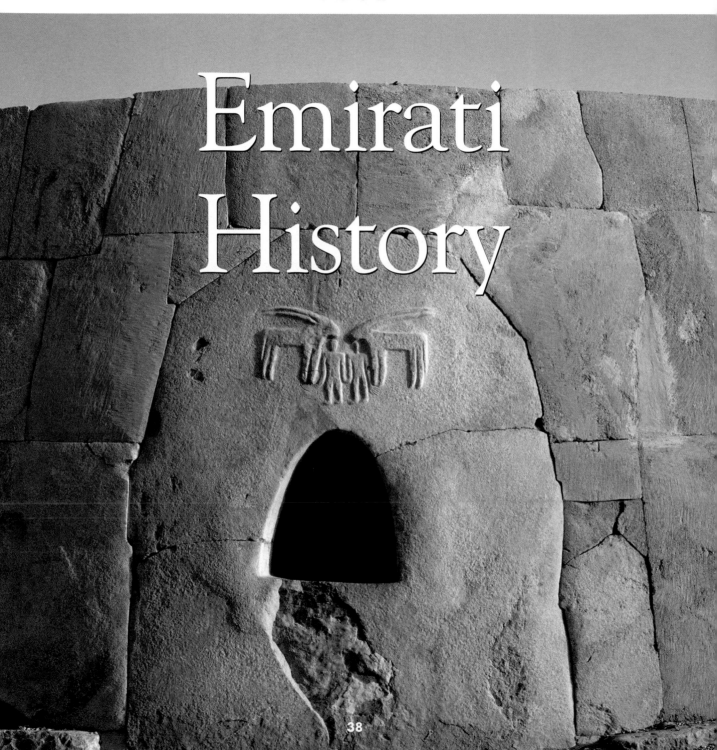

Emirati History

An archaeological site in
Ra's al-Khaimah

T HE ARABIAN PENINSULA HAS A LONG HUMAN HISTORY.
People first lived there many thousands of years ago. They established settlements in what is now the United Arab Emirates
by 3000 B.C.

One major settlement grew up on the island of Umm al-
Nar near Abu Dhabi. Tombs carved with pictures of camels
have been discovered at this site, which suggests that the
people living there kept camel herds. Other artifacts at Umm
al-Nar show that its ancient people fished, wove baskets, and
grew wheat. They also traded goods with faraway lands.

Opposite: **A tomb dating
back five thousand years
was uncovered near al-Ain
in the 1960s. It has since
been reconstructed.**

Ancient Tools

In July 2006, officials from Sharjah announced an important discovery. Archaeologists had uncovered a prehistoric workshop near the Hajar Mountains that had been used to make stone tools. Experts testing the tools concluded that they were made about one hundred thousand years ago. The tools suggest that humans lived in the area much earlier than had previously been believed.

Goods were transported on overland trade routes traveled by camel caravans. Sea trade was also important to the region's early peoples. Goods from India and China were shipped into the area. The main exports were pearls from the Persian Gulf. Later, the discovery of new ways to irrigate dry land allowed oasis settlements to grow and thrive.

The Prophet

In A.D. 630, representatives of the Prophet Muhammad arrived in southeastern Arabia. They brought an important message, one that would change the region forever. They explained that Muhammad was preaching a new religion based on messages he said he had received from God. At the time, the people of the Arabian Peninsula generally believed in many gods. But Muhammad said there was only one god. Muhammad's religion became known as Islam, and its followers came to be called Muslims. The people in what is now the UAE soon converted.

After the death of Muhammad in 632, leadership of the Muslims fell to Abu Bakr, who was given the title *caliph*, meaning "successor." Immediately, Caliph Abu Bakr set about crushing a revolt against his rule. The conflict ended with a battle at Dibba, a town in what is now al-Fujairah on the coast of the Gulf of Oman. With the defeat of the rebels, the caliph's control over Arabia was restored.

In the centuries that followed, the caliphs continued to spread Islam and expand their empire. In 637 and 892, their armies used the port of Julfar (now Ra's al-Khaimah) as a staging post for their conquests of present-day Iran and Oman. Julfar grew wealthy from serving as the center for the pearl trade. Fleets of dhows, large wooden ships used in trade throughout the region, plied the nearby waters.

Muslims believe that Muhammad received messages from God many times over the course of twenty-two years.

Ahmad ibn Majid

Ahmad ibn Majid is one of the most revered figures in Emirati history. He was both a brave sailor and a gifted poet. Ibn Majid was born in about 1432 in the coastal town of Julfar. In his writings, Ibn Majid told what he knew of navigation and geography. He wrote about forty works, nearly all in verse. One of the longest is the *Fawa'id*. In this poem, Ibn Majid describes his understanding of navigation and astronomy. He continued writing until his death in about 1500.

Europeans Arrive

In the late fifteenth century, a new group of traders began to arrive in the region. They were from the European country of Portugal. Portuguese explorer Vasco da Gama had discovered a sea route from Europe to the Indian Ocean when he sailed around the southern tip of Africa.

The traders in Arabia were not pleased to meet the Portuguese. They realized that these newcomers wanted to cut into their trading business. Fighting erupted, and in the early sixteenth century, the Portuguese took control of several coastal towns in what is now the UAE and imposed taxes on the local leaders.

The ruler of Persia (now Iran) grew tired of the situation. He allied himself with two other European countries, Great Britain and the Netherlands. These countries helped drive out the Portuguese in exchange for a cut of the money made in Persia's ports. But for the people of the Persian Gulf coast, this was only a partial victory. The Portuguese were gone, but now they had to deal with the British and the Dutch (the people of the Netherlands), both of whom wanted more control over the region.

Vasco da Gama found a sea route between Europe and Asia. This promoted trade between the two regions.

The Pirate Coast

Two powerful tribal groups, the Bani Yas and the Qawasim, emerged in the area in the eighteenth century. Today, most native Emiratis are descended from one of these two tribes.

The Bani Yas were originally farmers and herders who lived in the villages at Liwa Oasis. By the 1790s, however, the leader of the important al-Nahayan family moved to the coastal town of Abu Dhabi to take advantage of the pearling industry. A few decades later, another branch of the Bani Yas, the Al Bu Falasah, settled in Dubai.

The Qawasim were largely traders living in what are now the emirates of Sharjah and Ra's al-Khaimah. As their power grew, they built up a large fleet of ships. The Qawasim began attacking the British, who by then were dominating the coastal trade and had also taken control of large parts of India. The British called the attackers pirates and began calling the region the Pirate Coast.

By the beginning of the nineteenth century, the Qawasim had more than sixty large vessels and some twenty thousand sailors at their disposal. The British also had a powerful navy, and they began to wage an all-out war on the Qawasim

Al-Fihaidi

In Dubai is a beautiful building with walls embedded with shell and coral. It is al-Fihaidi Fort, and it may be the oldest building in the city. Al-Fihaidi was built in about 1787. When the city was attacked, people would crowd into it for protection. In recent years, the building has been restored. It is now home to the Dubai Museum.

pirates. The British wanted to gain control over trade in the region. To do this, they would have to defeat the Qawasim and drive their European competitors away. In 1819, the British succeeded in taking over the best harbors on the coast, including the pirate headquarters at Ra's al-Khaimah.

The British fought the Qawasim in the Persian Gulf in the early 1800s.

The Trucial Coast

A year later, the sheikhs (local leaders) of the Pirate Coast signed a peace treaty with the British. In it, the Qawasim promised to end their piracy. This was just the first of a series of agreements between the British and the sheikhs. In 1835, the two sides renewed their truce, and the sheikhs agreed to let the British police any fighting that broke out between their peoples. In 1853, both sides agreed to a permanent end to hostilities between them. With this treaty, the coastal sheikhdoms also got a new name—the Trucial Coast. This name arose because the sheikhdoms had reached a "perpetual maritime truce" with the British.

Even with this agreement in place, the British worried about other nations, such as France, Russia, and Germany, moving in on their interests in the Persian Gulf region. To make sure that the Trucial Coast did not deal with these nations, they proposed still another treaty, the "Exclusive Agreement," in 1892. By signing the treaty, the sheikhs agreed to allow Britain to conduct their foreign relations. The sheikhs were forbidden to sell land to any other nation or make treaties with any other nation. In exchange, the British were to provide military protection for the Trucial Coast. In all other ways, however, the sheikhs were left to rule their people as they saw fit.

Pearl divers used no special equipment. They simply held their breath, or sometimes pinned their noses closed, while they dived to the seafloor.

Pearls and Oil

At the beginning of the twentieth century, the people of the Trucial Coast relied largely on pearling for income and jobs. Many pearl divers were from the branch of the Bani Yas tribe that lived in Liwa. They spent their summers on pearling boats off the Persian Gulf coast and then returned to their desert oasis homes to tend their date-tree groves.

Pearling was vital to the region's economy until the 1930s, when a worldwide economic depression dried up the market for pearls. In the next decade, India imposed a heavy tax on pearls imported from the Gulf. This delivered the final death blow to the industry. The Trucial Coast grew poorer and poorer, leaving its people with little income and their society lacking the most basic services.

Sheikh Shakhbut bin Sultan al-Nahayan ruled Abu Dhabi for nearly forty years.

In time, the area's fortune's turned. In 1958, oil was found off the coast of Abu Dhabi. Within a few years, this sheikhdom became enormously rich. At first, this newfound wealth had little effect on the average resident of Abu Dhabi. Its reigning sheikh, Shakhbut bin Sultan al-Nahayan, was overly cautious about spending the oil income to help develop the sheikhdom. In 1966, the ruling family decided it was time for a change and replaced him with his younger brother, Sheikh Zayd bin Sultan al-Nahayan. Unlike his brother, Sheikh Zayd was eager to use Abu Dhabi's oil money to fund vast public works programs. Suddenly, all of Abu Dhabi was awash with construction projects. Everywhere, new homes, hospitals, schools, and roads were being built. After oil was discovered in Dubai in 1966, its ruler, Sheikh Rashid bin Sa'id al-Maktum, launched a similar campaign.

The Birth of the UAE

In the meantime, the British moved to change their relationship with the Trucial Coast sheikhdoms. In 1952, they recommended that the sheikhs create a trucial council to meet twice a year. The council was to establish policies that all the sheikhdoms would follow.

The formation of the council was the first step in a larger plan. In the nineteenth century, Britain had had a great empire that claimed land not just in the Persian Gulf region but over much of the world. But by the 1950s, Britain no longer had the money and military to police its old empire. The British had no choice but to give up control over lands such as the Trucial Coast.

In 1968, Britain announced that it would withdraw from the Trucial Coast in three years. Leaders in the region rushed to fill the political void created by the impending British withdrawal. They decided to form a new nation, the Federation of Arab Emirates. It was to include the Trucial Coast sheikhdoms and two other areas, Qatar and Bahrain, which had also been under British military protection. The federation was slated to become an independent state once the British left in 1971. But Qatar and Bahrain had second thoughts. They eventually decided to drop out and become separate countries of their own.

On December 2, 1971, the federation, now named the United Arab Emirates, declared its independence from Britain. The new country included six former sheikhdoms—Abu Dhabi, Ajman, al-Fujairah, Dubai, Sharjah, and Umm al-Qaiwain. Two months later, a seventh, Ra's al-Khaimah, joined the UAE. Sheikh Zayd, the leader of Abu Dhabi, was named president, and Sheikh Rashid, the ruler of Dubai, became vice president. His son, the crown prince of Dubai, Sheikh Maktum bin Rashid al-Maktum, was chosen to be the prime

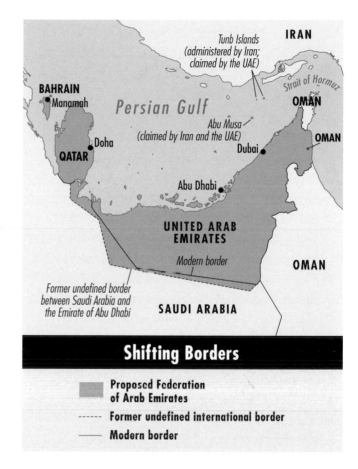

minister. These appointments reflected the importance of Abu Dhabi and Dubai, the two wealthiest emirates in the UAE.

Moving Forward

In its first three decades, the UAE was dominated by one figure—its president, Sheikh Zayd. From the start, governing the country was a challenge. The UAE had longstanding disputes with some of its neighbors. Iran seized control of three islands claimed by the UAE the day before it declared its

The Father of the UAE

The driving force behind the formation of the UAE, Sheikh Zayd bin Sultan al-Nahayan was born into the Bani Yas tribe in 1918. His father, Sheikh Sultan bin Zayd al-Nahayan, served as the ruler of Abu Dhabi from 1922 to 1926. After his father's death, young Zayd moved to the oasis of al-Ain, where he received his religious education. As an adult, he was chosen to govern al-Ain. In this role, he welcomed foreign oil companies, who discovered oil in Abu Dhabi in 1958.

Sheikh Zayd became the ruler of Abu Dhabi in 1966. Immediately, he set about using its oil income to develop the emirate. The sheikh oversaw the building of schools, housing, roads, bridges, and an airport. He also worked to establish a modern health care and educational system.

Two years after he took power, the British announced that they would withdraw from the region. Sheikh Zayd met with the leaders of neighboring emirates, pushing for them all to join together to form an independent nation. Largely because of his efforts, the UAE was

formed in 1971. He became president of the new country, a position he retained until his death in 2004. Sheikh Zayd is still revered and celebrated in the UAE as the father of the nation.

independence. But an even more daunting task was pulling all the Emirati people together. The emirates varied considerably in size and level of development. Many people outside the country doubted that the UAE leaders could work together to create a strong nation.

To their surprise, the UAE soon evolved into one of the most stable nations in the region. Sheikh Zayd's leadership deserves much of the credit. He drew on the Emirati tradition of governing through cooperation and made decisions that all the sheikhs could live with.

Sheikh Zayd also continued to funnel oil income into popular public works programs. Education became required for all Emirati children, and the UAE developed an excellent health care system. Sheikh Zayd oversaw the growth of new industries and the development of the UAE's ports as trade centers. In addition, he dedicated himself to causes he cared about. He used his position to promote traditional Emirati culture and to protect the nation's natural environment.

Sheikh Khalifa bin Zayd al-Nahayan is only the second president of the UAE.

Sheikh Zayd also proved an important force in international relations in the Middle East. Generally seen as a voice of moderation, he joined other nations in ousting Iraq's army from its neighbor Kuwait during the Gulf War (1991). Sheikh Zayd was also an outspoken critic of terrorism.

With Sheikh Zayd's death in 2004, his oldest son, Khalifa bin Zayd al-Nahayan, became president. Sheikh Khalifa has generally followed his father's policies. Entering the twenty-first century, he and the other leaders of the UAE are committed to continuing the work of those who came before. Together, they hope to preserve the nation's heritage while also leading their country into the future.

A Federation
of Emirates

In 1968, when the British announced that they were planning to withdraw from the Trucial Coast, the member sheikhdoms were faced with a big challenge. They needed to put together a national government that would replace British rule, and they needed to do it quickly.

At the time, each sheikhdom had its own government, ruled by a single man. That leader, the sheikh, was the head of the area's most powerful tribe. There were no written rules about how he should govern. Tradition held that a sheikh could keep his position only as long as his people respected him. In order to stay in touch with the concerns of the people, a sheikh was expected to hold regular meetings called *majlis*. At these councils, people could speak directly to the sheikh about their problems.

Opposite: **Emirati leaders talk during the creation of the United Arab Emirates in 1971.**

The National Flag

The national flag of the UAE features three horizontal stripes. They are green, white, and black. On the flag's left side is a wider vertical stripe in red. The same four colors, which represent Arab unity, also appear on the flags of many other Arab countries.

The sheikhs realized that to form a modern, independent nation, they needed a more formal and complex form of government. As the British were preparing to leave, the sheikhs quickly drew up a constitution. With this document, the United Arab Emirates was born.

The Constitution

The UAE constitution was adopted in 1971. Under this constitution, six of the former Trucial Coast sheikhdoms—Abu Dhabi, Dubai, Sharjah, Ajman, Umm al-Qaiwain, and al-Fujairah—became part of the new country. These sheikhdoms were from then on known as emirates. A seventh emirate, Ra's al-Khaimah, joined the UAE in February 1972.

According to the constitution, the new national government would have influence over areas that affect all the emirates. These areas include foreign affairs, defense, immigration, public health, education, and economic policy. The constitution states that any powers not specifically mentioned in the document would remain with the local government of each emirate. In this way, the constitution allows the emirates to retain their

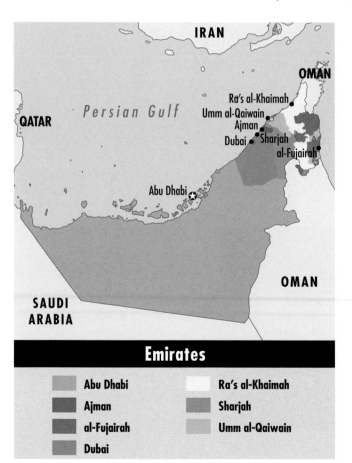

IRAN

OMAN

Persian Gulf

QATAR

Ra's al-Khaimah
Umm al-Qaiwain
Ajman
Dubai ● ● Sharjah
al-Fujairah ●

Abu Dhabi ☆

OMAN

SAUDI
ARABIA

Emirates

◼ Abu Dhabi		◻ Ra's al-Khaimah	
◼ Ajman		◼ Sharjah	
◼ al-Fujairah		◼ Umm al-Qaiwain	
◼ Dubai			

traditional governments while also participating in the new national government.

The Supreme Council of Rulers

By the terms of the UAE constitution, the most powerful body in the national government is the Supreme Council of Rulers. It is made up of the sheikhs of the seven emirates. These seven men are responsible for choosing the president and vice president. So far, the UAE has had two presidents and three vice presidents. The presidents have always been the rulers of Abu Dhabi, while the vice presidents have always been the rulers of Dubai.

Both officials serve five-year terms. After the term is up, the Supreme Council of Rulers can opt to renew their appointment. The first president of the UAE, Sheikh Zayd, served seven consecutive terms. His time as president ended only with his death in 2004.

The president has the job of choosing the prime minister, the head of state. With the help of the prime minister, he also selects his Council of Ministers. These officials head ministries (departments) charged with overseeing government policy in a variety of areas, including energy, labor, health, environment and water, and education. Since 2006, the Council of Ministers has had twenty-four members.

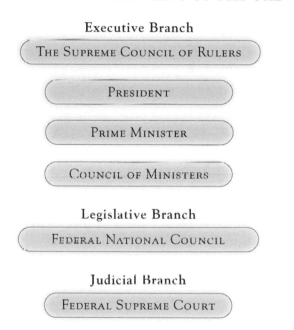

NATIONAL GOVERNMENT OF THE UAE

Executive Branch

The Supreme Council of Rulers

President

Prime Minister

Council of Ministers

Legislative Branch

Federal National Council

Judicial Branch

Federal Supreme Court

The Federal National Council reviews new laws, but it does not have the power to change them.

The Federal National Council

The Supreme Council of Rulers makes the laws in the UAE. But these laws must be approved by the Federal National Council (FNC). The FNC members also suggest changes in proposed laws and give formal approval of the president's choice of prime minister.

The FNC has forty members. They serve two-year terms. The size and population of each emirate determines how many people it sends to the council. Abu Dhabi and Dubai are represented by eight council members each; Sharjah and Ra's al-Khaimah, by six members each; and Ajman, Umm al-Qaiwain, and al-Fujairah, by four members each.

In the UAE, there are two types of courts. *Shari'a* courts are based on religion and rule on aspects of daily life. Civil courts deal primarily with business disputes.

The shari'a is a code of law based on the holy texts of Islam. It provides guidelines for just about every aspect of day-to-day life. The shari'a deals with both business and personal relationships, providing a legal framework for marriage, divorce, and other family matters. In addition, it establishes many rules of behavior. For instance, Muslims are forbidden to gamble, drink alcohol, eat pork, or dress immodestly. Applying the shari'a to everyday situations can be difficult. Judges in Islamic countries, therefore, are often religious scholars.

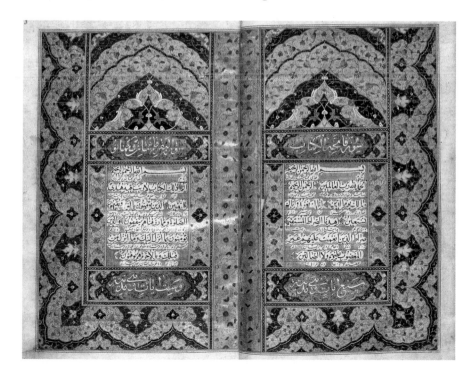

Shari'a law is based on the Qur'an and other holy texts.

In the UAE, shari'a courts hear family disputes and criminal cases. In criminal cases, however, a penal code is sometimes consulted if the shari'a does not cover a specific crime.

People accused of a crime in the UAE have the right to a trial. But they are not guaranteed a speedy trial, and since the UAE has no bail system, defendants sometimes wait in jail a long time before getting their day in court. The UAE legal system also has no juries. All cases are decided by judges.

Civil Courts

Lawsuits are first heard before local courts. A party that disputes a local court's verdict can contest the decision in the emirate's federal appeal court. A party that disagrees with

A guard keeps watch over prisoners in Dubai.

an appeal court's findings can take the case before the Federal Supreme Court, the highest court in the land.

The Federal Supreme Court is composed of five judges. They are appointed by the Supreme Council of Rulers. In addition to deciding appeals, the Supreme Court judges hear cases involving disagreements between the emirates. These cases may involve disputes over land or resources. The Supreme Court judges also make the final decision over whether contested local or federal laws are consistent with the UAE Constitution.

Federal judges are officially independent. They do not have to consider the wishes of important officials in making their decisions. But in practice, government officials have enormous sway over the judges. Many judges are from other countries, rather than being citizens of the UAE. If the president or another powerful political leader does not like a noncitizen judge, he can have the judge sent back to his homeland. Therefore, if judges want to keep their jobs and stay in the UAE, they have to be careful not to anger those in power.

"Long Live My Country"

The national anthem of the United Arab Emirates is "'A'ishi Biladi," meaning "Long Live My Country." Until 1996, the song had no lyrics. But after a national competition, 'Arif al Sheikh 'Abdullah al-Hasan provided the words, which Emiratis now sing to express their love for their nation.

> Live my country, the unity of our Emirates lives.
> You have lived for a nation,
> Whose religion is Islam and guide is the Qur'an,
> I made you stronger in God's name, oh homeland.
> My country, my country, my country, my country,
> God has protected you from the evils of the time.
> We have sworn to build and work.
> Work sincerely, work sincerely,
> As long as we live, we'll be sincere, sincere.
> The safety has lasted, and the flag has lived, oh our Emirates,
> The symbol of Arabism.
> We all sacrifice for you, we supply you with our blood.
> We sacrifice for you with our souls, oh homeland.

Local Governments

Each of the seven emirates has a government of its own. Abu Dhabi has the most complicated emirate government. That is hardly surprising, given that Abu Dhabi is the biggest emirate in terms of area, population, and oil wealth. In fact, the annual budget of the Abu Dhabi emirate's government is bigger than that of the federal government of the UAE.

The main governing body of Abu Dhabi is the Executive Council. It is overseen by the emirate's crown prince, a son of Abu Dhabi's ruler. He is aided by three ruler's representatives. Two oversee the emirate's Western Region and Eastern Region, while a third is charge of the island of Das, which is important to the emirate's oil industry. In addition, Abu Dhabi has a sixty-member National Consultative Council, which operates much like the Federal National Council. The emirate also runs government departments that are similar to the national government's ministries.

Ruling by Tradition

The government of each emirate plays an important role in the day-to-day lives of the people. But equally important are less formal governing institutions that existed well before the UAE was formed. These appeal especially to older, more traditional people who are uncomfortable with newer government institutions.

The rulers of the emirates still make a point of holding majlis from time to time. At these meetings, people can bring their complaints before their leaders. In the larger emirates, majlis are organized by senior members of the sheikh's family.

But in the smaller emirates, the ruler or the crown prince is likely to oversee the meetings himself. For instance, the ruler of al-Fujairah himself holds a majlis once a week.

Sheikhs also still use a traditional method of governing settlements in remote areas. They appoint a well-respected person from the most prominent tribe there as their local representative. The people who live in the settlement come to him with their problems and complaints. The local representative passes these on to the emirate's leadership. In this way, tribal people in areas far from the center of power can still have their voices heard.

Sheikh Khalifa

In 2004, Sheikh Khalifa bin Zayd al-Nahayan became the second president in the history of the UAE. Sheikh Khalifa, who was born in 1948, has been involved in national politics since the country was founded. Soon after his father, Sheikh Zayd, was chosen to be the UAE's first president in 1971, he named Sheikh Khalifa the deputy prime minister. Sheikh Khalifa continued to assist his father for the next three decades. He became especially important during Sheikh Zayd's final years, when his health was failing.

Like his father, Sheikh Khalifa has modernized his nation and improved people's standard of living. One of his earliest acts as president was to authorize a 25 percent salary increase for citizens working in the government. The president has also restructured the federal government to improve its efficiency.

A Stable Country

The UAE's system of government, which was cobbled together quickly in 1971, has proven surprisingly effective. In recent years, the country's population has skyrocketed and its economy has exploded. But even amid rapid change, the country's government has remained remarkably stable.

Perhaps the biggest test to the UAE's system of government came in 2004, with the death of President Zayd. Until that time, the popular Zayd had been the country's only president. With President Zayd gone, the leaders of the various emirates might have begun fighting among themselves, jockeying to fill the former president's shoes. But instead, just an hour after President Zayd died, the Supreme Council of Rulers announced that it had elected Zayd's son, Sheikh Khalifa bin

In December 2006, a woman votes in the first election ever held in the UAE. Although only a few thousand voters were able to take part in the election, it was a small step toward reform.

Zayd Al-Nahayan, as the new president. This smooth transition was possible in part because the Supreme Council of Rulers was already comfortable with Sheikh Khalifa and trusted his leadership. In addition to serving as the crown prince of Abu Dhabi for more than thirty years, he had also taken over many of his father's duties during the end of his rule.

Sheikh Khalifa made clear that he wanted to continue his father's policies. But in December 2005, he announced that it was time to make some reforms. Since the country's founding, the members of the FNC had been chosen by the Supreme Council of Rulers. The president wanted a broader group, more representative of the nation at large, to select at least some of these important officials.

President Khalifa decreed that each emirate should form an electoral college. Each electoral college would hold an election to choose half of that emirate's FNC members. The other half would still be chosen by the Supreme Council of Rulers.

President Khalifa's decree led to the first election in the history of the UAE. In December 2006, more than six thousand electoral college members voted twenty representatives into the FNC. The historic election was a small step toward allowing Emiratis to have more say in their government. President Khalifa expressed hope that it would help educate his people about how elections work. He also holds open the possibility that one day the citizens of the UAE will elect the entire Federal National Council and that the council will be given the power not just to advise the sheikhs about proposed laws but to write the laws themselves.

Abu Dhabi: Did You Know This?

Abu Dhabi, the glittering capital of the UAE, is one of the richest cities in the world. It is located on an island in the Persian Gulf.

With an estimated population of 552,000 people, Abu Dhabi is the UAE's second-largest city. Because Abu Dhabi Emirate has most of the nation's oil, Abu

Dhabi City is the center of its oil industry as well as the home of the national government. The wealth of Abu Dhabi is obvious from its tall skyscrapers, busy streets, and lush public parks and gardens. One of the most popular sites in Abu Dhabi is the Corniche, a lovely waterfront park that was refurbished in 2005.

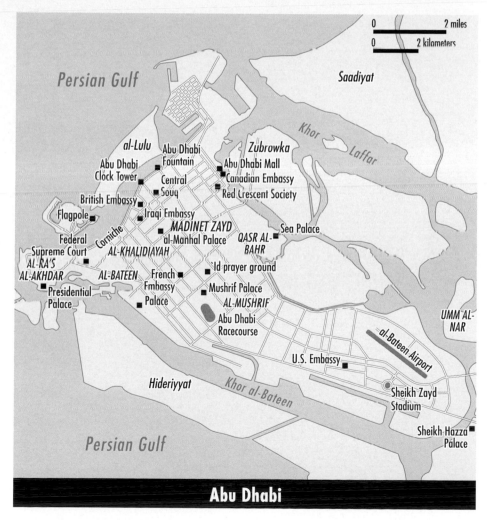

0   2 miles
0   2 kilometers

Persian Gulf

Saadiyat

Khor Laffar

al-Lulu

Abu Dhabi Clock Tower

Abu Dhabi Fountain

Zubrowka

Abu Dhabi Mall

Canadian Embassy

Central Souq

Red Crescent Society

British Embassy

Flagpole

Iraqi Embassy

MADINET ZAYD

al-Manhal Palace

QASR AL-BAHR

Sea Palace

Corniche

Federal Supreme Court

AL-KHALIDIAYAH

AL-RA'S AL-AKHDAR

AL-BATEEN

French Embassy Palace

Id prayer ground

Mushrif Palace

AL-MUSHRIF

UMM AL-NAR

Presidential Palace

Abu Dhabi Racecourse

al-Bateen Airport

U.S. Embassy

Hideriyyat

Khor al-Bateen

Sheikh Zayd Stadium

Persian Gulf

Sheikh Hazza Palace

Abu Dhabi

A Booming
Economy

O NLY A FEW DECADES AGO, THE PEOPLE OF WHAT IS NOW the UAE led humble lives. Most made a living by farming, fishing, or raising animals. In the summer, many men went to the coastal region to work as pearl divers in the hope of making a little extra money.

In the late 1950s and early 1960s, everything began to change. Large reserves of oil were discovered in Abu Dhabi and smaller reserves were found in Dubai, Ra's al-Khaimah, and Sharjah. Since then, the oil industry and the money it provides Emiratis have completely transformed the UAE's economy. The UAE now boasts one of the highest standards of living in the region. In fact, the Emiratis' quality of life is on par with many nations in North America and Europe.

The Oil Industry

In 2006, the UAE produced about 3 percent of the world's crude oil. The vast majority of it came from Abu Dhabi Emirate. According to the UAE's constitution, each emirate controls its own oil income.

Opposite: **The United Arab Emirates produces 2.5 million barrels of oil a day.**

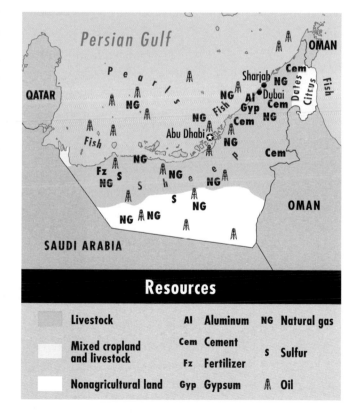

Persian Gulf

QATAR

OMAN

Sharjah
Dubai
Abu Dhabi

OMAN

SAUDI ARABIA

Resources

Livestock	Al Aluminum NG Natural gas
Mixed cropland and livestock	Cem Cement S Sulfur Fz Fertilizer
Nonagricultural land	Gyp Gypsum Oil

As a result, Abu Dhabi is not only the largest but also the wealthiest emirate in the UAE.

The UAE also has vast reserves of natural gas. It has the fifth-largest supply of natural gas in the world. As with oil, most of the UAE's natural gas reserves are located in Abu Dhabi.

Oil and natural gas will no doubt be an important part of the UAE's economy far into the future. By current estimates, the country has enough oil to last 150 years and enough gas to last 200 years.

Investing in the Economy

The UAE's leaders are looking to broaden the economy beyond the oil industry. Although they can rely on oil income

Emirati Money

The basic unit of currency in the United Arab Emirates is the dirham. It is equal in value to 100 fils. Coins come in values of 1 dirham and 1, 5, 10, 25, and 50 fils. Paper money comes in values of 5, 10, 20, 50, 100, 500, and 1,000 dirhams. In June 2007, US$1 equaled 3.67 dirhams, and 1 dirham equaled 27¢.

The pictures on UAE paper money celebrate landmarks, places, activities, animals, and objects important to the nation's history and culture. For example, the front of the 50-dirham bill shows the head of an oryx, while the back shows Fort Jahili in al-Ain.

for many decades, they realize that one day the reserves will dry up. As a result, they are working to develop other industries that will benefit all the people of the UAE.

To encourage industry, they had to improve the country's infrastructure. Before the discovery of oil, the UAE had almost no paved roads. Now, all the emirates are connected by a vast road network.

The nation has also invested in its ports so that goods can easily be shipped in and out of the country. The UAE has a growing shipbuilding industry. Its showpiece will be Dubai Maritime City, which is scheduled for completion in 2011. Dubai Maritime City will house many shipbuilding and ship repair companies.

The UAE is proud of its successful investment in the aviation industry. The country has six international airports, making it a major transportation hub between Europe and

Water transportation is vital to the UAE's economy.

Foreign Workers

In today's UAE, most Emirati citizens live fairly comfortable lives. Some are wealthy. Many receive financial aid from the government. All citizens receive free education and health care.

The foreign workers who make up most of the population of the UAE are not so lucky. About 60 percent are poor Asians who came to the country to work and, hopefully, to send money back home to their impoverished families. Some borrowed money to pay for the work visas needed to enter the UAE.

Once in the UAE, many foreign workers' dreams are dashed. Most can find only low-paying work as domestic servants, taxi drivers, and day laborers. Some have trouble getting the paychecks they have been promised, which they need to pay back their visa loans. Others are abused by their employers or forced to work under terrible conditions. Construction workers, for instance, commonly labor outside in suffocating heat, earning only about US$5 a day for twelve hours of backbreaking work.

Human rights organizations have recently taken up the cause of these workers. The workers themselves have started staging protests to draw attention to their plight. Under pressure, local governments have made some moves to improve the lives of foreign workers. In Dubai, for instance, employers are forbidden to force laborers to work outdoors during the hottest hours in July and August.

Southeast Asia. Following the completion of an enormous expansion project, the Abu Dhabi International Airport alone will be able to service fifty million passengers a year. The UAE is home to several airlines. Among them is Emirates Airlines, based in Dubai. It is one of the top ten airlines in the world, both in terms of the number of passengers it serves and the number of miles its planes fly each year.

Another challenge facing the Emirati economy is its labor force. With its explosive growth, the UAE has had to import workers from other countries. In fact, foreigners now make up more than 90 percent of the nation's workers. Most Emirati citizens in the labor force work for the government. Only about 2 percent of employed Emiratis work for private companies.

More and more Emirati citizens are taking advantage of the educational opportunities available to them. The government is making reforms to ensure that new graduates can get good jobs. Its leaders are beginning to make private companies set aside a certain number of positions for people who are legal citizens of the UAE.

Use of the UAE's airports is skyrocketing. The number of passengers at Dubai International Airport more than tripled between 1997 and 2006.

Goats and sheep are the most common livestock in the UAE.

Agriculture

The one industry dominated by native-born workers is agriculture. The Emiratis have a long tradition of farming. People in the region have been growing crops for at least 7,500 years.

But the way they farm has changed in recent years. The leaders of the UAE have poured large sums of money into agriculture. They hope that some day the nation will be able to produce much, if not all, of its own food. As a result, even though most farms are fairly small, farming in the UAE is a well-paying profession.

Farmers face many challenges growing crops in the UAE. High temperatures, poor soil, and limited water resources make farming difficult. The government helps out by providing

What the United Arab Emirates Grows, Makes, and Mines

Agriculture (2000)

Tomatoes	780,000 metric tons
Dates	318,000 metric tons
Meat	89,000 metric tons

Manufacturing

Cement (2005 est.)	9,800,000 metric tons
Aluminum (2006)	861,000 metric tons
Urea (2006 est.)	678,000 metric tons

Mining

Oil (2006)	2.8 million barrels a day
Natural gas (2005)	65 billion cubic meters

farmers with free seeds, pesticides, and irrigation systems as well as special training and equipment. Farmers who raise livestock also get free veterinarian services. Because of the government's efforts, more land is farmed in the UAE now than ever before. From the mid-1970s to 2002, the amount of farmland in the country rose from 37,000 acres (15,000 hectares) to 657,000 acres (266,000 ha).

Fishing with Technology

People have been fishing in the Persian Gulf for thousands of years. Today, many fishers use modern methods to ensure the best catch. In the past, fishers placed fish cages woven from palm fronds on the seabed, marking their location with buoys floating on the water's surface. Emiratis still use fish cages today, but they are made from steel wire. Many people have given up using buoys because poachers can spot them and steal their catch. Instead, they make note of where their underwater cages are with the Global Positioning System (GPS), which uses satellites to find exact spots on Earth's surface. With no markers on the water's surface, fish thieves can't find the cages.

The most important food grown in the UAE is dates, one of the favorite foods in the Middle East. The UAE now grows enough dates to produce all it needs and still export to other nations. Other leading crops include citrus fruits and mangoes. Farms that raise cows and chickens also produce dairy products and eggs.

Factories and Manufacturing

Agriculture is not the only industry supported by the UAE government. The country's leaders are also trying to transform the UAE into a manufacturing center. At first, manufacturing in the UAE concentrated on products made from gas and oil, such as chemicals and fertilizers. More recently, it has branched out. Among the products now made in the UAE are electronics, machinery, security equipment, medical equipment, air conditioners, and sporting equipment.

The UAE owes much of its manufacturing success to Sheikh Maktum bin Rashid al-Maktum, who was vice president of the UAE from 1990 to 2006. In 1985, when Sheikh Maktum was crown prince

Men build a submarine at a factory in Dubai. Manufacturing in the UAE has grown rapidly in recent years.

Workers recycle steel in the Jabal Ali Free Trade Zone.

of Dubai, he established the Jabal Ali Free Trade Zone 30 miles (50 km) from Dubai City. Maktum lured foreign companies to set up shop in the area with several promises. He told them that they could fully own their firms there. (Outside the free trade zone, citizens of the UAE must own at least 51 percent of each manufacturing facility.) He also said that the companies would not have to pay any income tax. The deal has convinced about fifteen hundred companies to go into business in the zone. This includes some two hundred factories, including ones operated by Reebok, Xerox, Sony, and Honda.

The enormous success of the Jabal Ali Free Trade Zone has led the UAE to establish dozens more. Many are meant to help specific industries. For instance, in Dubai alone, trade zones include Dubai Internet City, Dubai Media City, and Dubai Healthcare City.

The UAE is filled with hotels that cater to wealthy tourists. The luxurious Burj al-Arab Hotel sits on an artificial island near the beach in Dubai.

The UAE also is busy developing service industries. In fact, more than half the workers in the country are employed in the service sector. In Abu Dhabi, the most important industry after oil production is banking and financial services. In Dubai, leading industries include telecommunications and real estate sales.

The fastest-growing industry in the UAE, however, is tourism. Dubai City has been especially successful at reinventing itself as a paradise for tourists and business travelers. More than five million people from around the world visit Dubai every year. The city is especially popular with visitors from India, Pakistan, Iran, Lebanon, Australia, South Africa, the Philippines, and many countries in Europe. Today, tourism brings more money into Dubai than the oil industry does.

The leaders of Dubai decided to focus on its tourist industry in the 1980s. While Dubai has oil reserves, they are not large enough to keep the emirate wealthy forever. But Dubai's other natural resources make it a natural tourist destination. It offers travelers long sandy beaches, warm seas rich in marine life, and a pleasant climate for much of the year. And with air-conditioning, indoor complexes and hotels can be made comfortable even when the weather outside is blisteringly hot.

Today, Dubai has much more than its natural wonders to attract visitors. It is filled with luxury hotels, giant shopping malls, world-class restaurants, and enormous theme parks. As the Dubai tourism industry has bloomed, one idea seems to have guided the city: bigger is always better. Today, Dubai counts among its many attractions the Burj al-Arab, the world's tallest hotel, and the Mall of the Emirates, the biggest shopping mall in the Middle East.

Guests take slices of a massive ice cream cake in Dubai in 1999. The cake measured 53 feet (16 m) long.

To attract tourists during the hottest weeks of the summer, the city has also taken to featuring some strange and record-breaking objects. For instance, in the summer of 1999, Dubai proudly displayed the longest gold chain ever made (stretching 2.6 miles [4.2 km]) and an ice-cream cake the size of a swimming pool.

Dubai's extraordinary success in the tourism industry has inspired the other emirates. Abu Dhabi launched an ambitious long-term program to draw tourists. One project is the development of Saadiyat Island into a resort, with two dozen hotels and a branch of the Guggenheim Museum, a leading art museum based in New York. Abu Dhabi's efforts to expand its tourist industry have already begun to pay off. In the first half of 2006 alone, tourism in the emirate increased by 17 percent.

Visitors come from all over the world to relax at the resorts in the UAE.

Sharjah has chosen a different way of drawing in visitors. It plays up its many museums and cultural attractions. These hold a special appeal to Arabs throughout the Gulf region who want to learn more about their culture.

The natural beauties of Ra's al-Khaimah have also proven popular with travelers. Tourists now flock to luxury hotels and resorts nestled in the emirate's mountains. The emirate also plans to create an attraction more out of this world than anything in Dubai. A company called Space Adventures hopes to build a space port in the emirate, from which the wealthiest and most adventurous tourists could ride a spacecraft 60 miles (100 km) into the sky.

This wind tower and watch-tower are among the many historic sites in Sharjah.

Natives and
Foreigners

IN 2005, THE GOVERNMENT OF THE UAE INITIATED AN ambitious project—an in-depth national census. More than one thousand census takers traveled all over the country to count the people living there. They compiled a wealth of information about the people who call the UAE their home.

According to the 2005 census, the country's population is approximately 3,769,000. (This figure does not include some 335,600 noncitizen residents who were not in the UAE at the time the census was taken.) The census confirmed that the number of people living in the UAE had exploded in recent years. Since 1995, when the last census was taken, the population increased by about 75 percent.

The Population Boom

The staggering economic growth of the UAE accounts for this booming population. Only about 22 percent of the population are UAE nationals. The rest are immigrants who come to the UAE to work. They were attracted by the wide range of jobs in manufacturing, construction, tourism, and other industries available in Abu Dhabi and Dubai.

Because of the large number of foreign workers, the population of the UAE is unusually diverse for a Middle Eastern nation. About half the foreigners in the UAE are from South Asia and Southeast Asia.

Emirate Populations

The 2005 census found that Abu Dhabi has the largest population—1,292,119—of the seven emirates. Close behind is Dubai, with a population of 1,200,309. The rest of the five emirates have a total population of just 1,276,652.

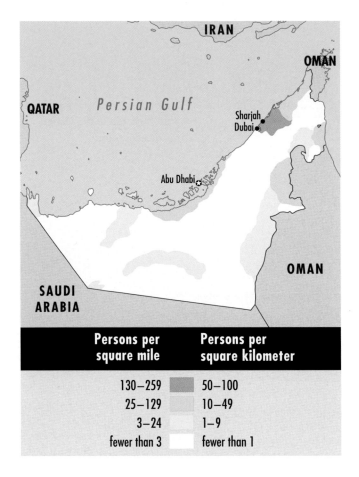

Persons per square mile		Persons per square kilometer
130–259		50–100
25–129		10–49
3–24		1–9
fewer than 3		fewer than 1

Ethnic Groups in the UAE

Emiratis (primarily Arabs)	19%
Other Arabs and Iranians	23%
South Asians	50%
Other non-Emiratis (including Europeans, East Asians, and Americans)	8%

Many also come from Arab nations such as Egypt, Jordan, Yemen, Oman, and the Palestinian territories. The rest come primarily from Iran, Afghanistan, and various European countries.

A Wealthy Nation

There is little poverty in the UAE. With its economic growth, most people who want to work and are able to can find a job. The generosity of the government also nearly guarantees Emiratis a good standard of living. Many citizens' housing costs are paid in full or in part by the government. Their children are entitled to a free education in public schools from kindergarten through college.

The government also sends out monthly checks to about seventy-seven thousand citizens who might otherwise have a hard time getting by. These checks are given to the elderly, orphans, divorced women, widows, married students, and the disabled. Because the cost of living was rising fast, President Khalifa increased these payments by 75 percent in 2005.

All these benefits are limited to UAE citizens, however. Workers from other countries do not get free education, health care, or other services.

The Bedouin

The vast majority of people in the UAE are city dwellers. But in the desert lands of Abu Dhabi live tribal people known as Bedouin. While some Bedouin have moved to cities to find work, many continue to live as their ancestors did for hundreds of years. The Bedouin primarily herd camels and other animals. They spend their days roaming the desert, looking for grazing lands for their animals.

Population of the Largest Cities (2003)

Dubai	1,171,000
Abu Dhabi	552,000
Sharjah	519,000
Al-Ain	348,000
Ajman	225,000

Young Emiratis march in a parade in Abu Dhabi.

Overall, the UAE has a young population. The majority of Emiratis—51 percent of them—are less than twenty years old. Noncitizens are somewhat older. About 49 percent are between twenty-five and forty years old. Recent improvements in health care allow people in the UAE to live longer than ever. The average life expectancy today is seventy-seven years.

Emirati citizens are about evenly divided between males and females. But among noncitizens living in the UAE, there are three men for every woman. As a result, the population as a whole is 68 percent male and 32 percent female.

A female trader watches the numbers change at the stock exchange in Abu Dhabi. More and more Emirati women are getting jobs.

On average, a woman in the UAE has slightly more than two children. Traditionally, many Emirati mothers stayed home to take care of their children while their husbands earned the family's sole income. Since the federation was formed, however, the position of women has been changing. The UAE Constitution grants women the same rights as men, and recent laws help protect them against discrimination in the workplace. These legal protections, as well as new educational opportunities, have inspired more women to work outside the home. In 1995, just 5 percent of Emirati women held jobs. A decade later, the number had risen to 16 percent.

Emirati Names

Bin ("son of") and *bint* ("daughter of") often appear in Emirati names. For instance, the name of President Khalifa bin Zayd al-Nahayan means "Khalifa, son of Zayd al-Nahayan."

Emirati children begin school at age six.

Arabic is the official language of the UAE. It is written using the twenty-eight-character Arabic alphabet. In written Arabic, words read from right to the left.

So many people from other countries live in the UAE that anyone walking down a city street is likely to hear conversations in English, Urdu, Hindi, or Persian. Employees of foreign companies in the UAE often do business in English. The government is now working to see that more of its citizens learn that language. In public schools, English instruction begins in kindergarten.

Common Arabic Words and Phrases

Al salaam alaykum	Hello
Ma' al-salama	Good-bye
Tisbah ala-khayr (to a man)	
Tisbihin ala-khayr (to a woman)	Good night
Fursa sa'ida.	Pleased to meet you.
Kif al-hal?	How are you?
Kif al-'a'ila?	How is your family?
Baraka Allah bik	Thank you
Afwan.	You're welcome.

Literacy is a high priority. In 1975, only 54 percent of Emirati men and 31 percent of Emirati women could read and write. But with the government's aggressive campaign to provide educational opportunities for its people, the literacy rate for citizens has risen quickly. Recent estimates claim that 84 percent of men and 91 percent of women are literate.

A child practices writing Arabic.

Faith in the Emirates

Each year, more than two million Muslims make a pilgrimage to Mecca.

W HEN THE UAE WAS FORMED IN 1971, ITS NEW CON-
stitution named Islam as the country's official religion. By that
time, Islam had been practiced by the people in the region for
more than thirteen centuries. It was first introduced to what
is now the UAE in the seventh century and has been a domi-
nant force in the lives of the people there ever since.

Opposite: **Muslims bow
towards Mecca, the holiest
city in Islam, when they pray.**

The Prophet

Islam arose from the preaching of the Prophet Muhammad. In 570, Muhammad was born in Mecca, a city in present-day Saudi Arabia. Muslims believe that when Muhammad was about forty years old, he was visited by the angel Gabriel. The angel brought him messages from God (*Allah* in Arabic).

Muhammad began to tell others in Mecca about his religious experience. At the time, most of the people of Mecca worshipped more than one god, so his insistence that there was only one god was a radical message. Soon, Muhammad attracted followers. They wrote down what Allah had told him, which included instructions on how to live a good and moral life. These words were later compiled in the holy book of Islam, which is called the Qur'an.

Most Muslims memorize parts of the Qur'an.

As more and more people became followers of Muhammad, the authorities in Mecca became concerned that Muhammad had too much power. As a result, the Prophet fled the city. He headed north to the city of Medina in 622, on a journey now known as the *Hijra*. In Medina, Muhammad continued to spread the word of Allah until his return to Mecca in triumph in 630. He died in 632.

The Five Pillars

Islam is the second largest religion in the world after Christianity. There are about 1.2 billion Muslims around the globe. They all follow religious duties known as the Five Pillars of Islam:

- *Shahadah* calls on Muslims to make the following statement of faith: "There is no god but God, and Muhammad is the prophet of God."
- *Salat* requires them to pray five times a day.
- *Zakat* obliges them to give money to the poor.
- *Sawm* commands them to fast in the month of Ramadan.
- *Hajj* requires all who are able to travel to the holy city of Mecca once in their lives.

Salat has the greatest effect on the day-to-day lives of Emirati Muslims. Five times throughout the day, they stop whatever they are doing to pray. Muslims follow certain traditions when performing their daily prayers. They kneel facing in the direction of Mecca while reciting from the Qur'an. By touching their heads to the floor, they show their complete submission to Allah.

Faith in the Emirates **91**

Men at a mosque in Dubai wait to break their fast during Ramadan.

Like other Muslims, those in the UAE observe the fast of Ramadan, the ninth month of the Islamic calendar. Throughout the month of Ramadan, Muslims fast during the daylight hours. They eat only a morning meal before the sun comes up and an evening meal after the sun goes down. During Ramadan, Muslims often devote extra time to reading the Qur'an or visiting mosques.

At the end of Ramadan, Muslim Emiratis celebrate 'Id al-Fitr. This three-day festival is a joyous time, shared by family and friends. People exchange gifts and gather together to enjoy eating all the rich foods they missed most during Ramadan.

Another important religious holiday in the UAE is 'Id al-Adha, a somber festival commemorating the willingness of the prophet Ibrahim (called Abraham in the Bible) to sacrifice his son for Allah. Emiratis also celebrate the Islamic New Year, the birthday of Muhammad, and the anniversary of the day the Prophet rose into heaven.

A man buys a goat for 'Id al-Adha. During this festival, Muslims slaughter goats to commemorate Ibrahim's willingness to sacrifice his son.

Sunnis and Shi'is

While nearly all UAE citizens are Muslims, they belong to two different groups within Islam—Sunnis and Shi'is. These groups emerged soon after the death of Muhammad amid arguments over who should succeed him as the leader of Islam. Shi'is believe the leader of Islam should be a direct descendant of the Prophet himself. Sunnis accept others.

Today, Sunnis make up about 80 percent of the world's Muslims. Among Muslim UAE citizens, 85 percent are Sunnis. The other 15 percent are Shi'is.

Most Emirati citizens are Arab Muslims, but many people of different faiths and backgrounds also live in the UAE.

The government of the UAE or an emirate government appoints and pays the salaries of the Sunni clergy, who are known as imams. Nearly all Sunni mosques also receive government funding.

Shi'i leaders are not given this kind of support, and their mosques are generally funded by private donors. The government does sometimes help a Shi'i imam financially if he makes a special request.

Government-funded schools teach about Islam along with other subjects.

Islam and the Government

In the UAE, the government encourages the practice of Islam through its educational system. Public schools are required to teach Islamic studies, and they are forbidden to teach about any other religion. Muslim students in private schools must also take lessons in Islamic traditions and principles.

Religion in the UAE

Citizens

Islam	96%
Other	4%

Noncitizens

Islam	55%
Hinduism	25%
Christianity	10%
Buddhism	5%
Other	5%

Islam is also at the center of the country's legal system. Laws in the UAE must be in keeping with the shari'a. The shari'a law applies to both criminal acts and personal behavior. For example, the shari'a forbids Muslim women to marry non-Muslim men.

Tolerating Other Faiths

Islam is not the only faith practiced by the people of the UAE. Although nearly all citizens are Muslim, only about 55 percent of foreigners in the UAE practice Islam. Most of the other noncitizens are Hindus, Christians, and Buddhists.

Compared with most countries in the Middle East, the UAE is fairly tolerant towards non-Muslims. They are usually allowed to worship as they wish, without interference.

Christians pray in front of a statue of the Virgin Mary in Dubai. It is estimated that more than three hundred thousand Christians live in the UAE.

A young child sits on Santa's lap in a mall in Dubai.

The UAE is particularly broad-minded in its regard for Christianity. There are more than thirty churches in the UAE. They are built on land donated by the government.

Churches in the UAE are allowed to advertise holiday celebrations and fund-raising events. In recent years, many stores with Christian clients have put up Christmas and Easter decorations. During the Christmas season in the giant malls of Dubai, it is even common to hear choirs singing carols and to see men dressed up as Santa Claus.

The Jumairah Mosque

Dubai City is home to the Jumairah Mosque. This modern structure, made from gleaming, cream-colored stone, was constructed using centuries-old traditions of mosque architecture. The elegant mosque is the only one in the UAE that welcomes non-Muslim visitors. The Sheikh Muhammad Center for Cultural Understanding organizes tours of the mosque to promote religious understanding and tolerance among people of all religions.

Non-Muslims in the UAE are expected to show respect for Islamic religious traditions. For instance, they tend to dress modestly, as the Qur'an commands. Non-Muslims also refrain from eating and drinking in public in daylight hours during the holy month of Ramadan.

Like every other Muslim nation, the UAE has laws that regulate the behavior of non-Muslims. One law makes it a crime for non-Muslims to try to convert Muslims to another religion or to distribute information about their religion. The government, meanwhile, actively encourages people of other religions to convert to Islam. Islam is so important in Emirati life that the government publishes an annual list of the previous year's converts.

A man walks by a modern mosque in Abu Dhabi.

CHAPTER

NINE

Arts and Sports

RAPID CHANGES IN THE UAE IN RECENT YEARS HAVE made the country exciting and prosperous. But they have also given the older generations cause for concern. Many older Emiratis, including some prominent leaders, fear that traditions may be forgotten and lost forever.

To keep this from happening, the government is working hard to preserve what it defines as traditional Emirati culture.

Opposite: **Celebrations in the UAE typically include music and dancing.**

Talking, relaxing, and drinking tea are central to Emirati culture.

Museums and historical sites throughout the country are devoted to introducing the old ways to both visitors to the country and young Emiratis. Schools also play an important role in keeping Emirati culture alive. They are required to teach students about the traditional Emirati arts of music, dance, and poetry.

Children learn traditional dances at schools in the UAE.

Traditional Arts

Until recently, most Emiratis could not read or write. Consequently, storytelling was a popular art. Among desert tribes, men would meet in the evening to chat and exchange news. During these times, one man in the group would often begin telling an old story or a legend to entertain his friends.

Poetry was also a favorite form of entertainment. Good poets were highly respected among the Emirati tribes. They especially enjoyed poets who recited verses that celebrated their own tribe while making fun of rival groups.

For as long as Emiratis can remember, song and dance have been part of their culture. At weddings and other celebrations, they perform dances that have been passed down from

Some Emirati dances date back thousands of years. In this traditional dance, women twirl their hair.

The 'ayyala dance is meant to look like a battle. Men move forward and backward, much like they advance and retreat in battle.

generation to generation. At these functions, men and women always dance separately. The *na'ahsat* is a women's dance. When performing it, a dancer places her right hand on her chest while swaying from side to side. Men often dance the 'ayyala. To the beat of a drum, rows of male 'ayyala dancers wave swords or sticks, playing out a mock battle. Aside from drums, traditional Emirati instruments include a flute called the *nai* and a stringed instrument known as the *rababa*.

Songs were once an important part of the pearling industry. Ships often hired a professional to sing as they sailed into the Persian Gulf. The other men would join in the song, which rallied them to work hard to find as many pearls as they could.

Preserving the Past

In addition to keeping traditional art forms alive, Emiratis are also preserving their heritage by protecting historical sites. Throughout the UAE, governments are restoring old buildings. In Dubai alone, plans are underway to repair more than three hundred historic structures by 2010.

Some historic buildings now house museums. In fact, the UAE has a museum devoted to just about any subject you could name. There are museums about science, aviation,

Ahlam

Ahlam 'Ali al-Shamsi is a popular singer throughout the Middle East. She was born in Bahrain in 1969 and became a UAE citizen at age twenty-seven. When she was a girl, she made a name for herself as a professional wedding singer. Even today, she sometimes sings at weddings for a fee of US$50,000. Known to her fans by just her first name, Ahlam has recorded nine CDs and is one of the most highly paid singers in the Arab world.

jewelry, natural history, Islam, astronomy, medicine, coins, and the discovery of oil in the region.

One of the most impressive historic buildings in the country is al-Husn. Located in the emirate of Sharjah, the structure was originally built in 1820 as the home of the emirate's ruling family. In 1969, the building was slated to be torn down. The emirate's current leader, Sheikh Sultan bin Muhammad al-Qasimi, was then a student in Egypt. When he found out that

Al-Ain National Museum

The city of al-Ain is home to al-Ain National Museum. The museum boasts that it covers seven thousand years of history. It houses many ancient treasures that were uncovered at the archaeological sites of Umm al-Nar and Qattarah. Among the objects on display are gold pendants in the shape of animals that date back four thousand years, and a collection of silver and bronze coins.

the beautiful palace was being destroyed, he rushed home and stopped the demolition. Though only a few walls were still standing, the sheikh decided to rebuild al-Husn. Supervising the project himself, he collected old photographs and consulted with elderly relatives to make sure every detail in the new al-Husn was just right.

Largely because of Sheikh Sultan's efforts, Sharjah is considered the cultural center of the UAE. The city includes a "Heritage Area," which is full of restored historic buildings and is home to the Sharjah Heritage Museum. Sharjah also features a vibrant arts community. Its galleries and theaters provide an environment where Emirati artists can explore arts that aren't part of Emirati tradition, such as painting, sculpture, and contemporary plays.

The Sharjah Heritage Museum is a group of museums that includes a restored market and family home. Displays include traditional clothes, crafts, and jewelry.

People enjoy a number of different water sports in the waters near Dubai.

Sports in the UAE

The UAE is not just known for its cultural sites. It is also famous as a great sports center. In many ways, the UAE is an ideal place for sports lovers. For much of the year, the sunny climate allows for outdoor sports. Throughout the country, people flock to parks and fields to play soccer, basketball, and rugby.

People living along the Gulf coast can also enjoy an array of water sports. Every weekend, natives and tourists trek to the beach. Some come to swim and lie in the sun. Others take to the water on Jet Skis and surfboards. Sailing is growing in popularity as well.

The UAE's varied landscape appeals to people who enjoy adventurous sports. They can go climbing in the mountains or ride camels in the desert. The UAE's eastern coast is especially exciting for snorkelers and scuba divers. There, in the waters of the Gulf of Oman, they can swim among fish and beautiful coral reefs.

The UAE has been successful in establishing itself as a destination spot for golfers. The country boasts several well-known golf courses. They are known not only for their challenging courses but also for their spectacular clubhouses. At the Abu Dhabi Golf Club, the clubhouse is in the shape of a falcon swooping down on a golf ball, while the clubhouse of the Dubai Creek Golf and Yacht Club looks like the sails of a dhow, a traditional wooden boat.

The first golf course in the UAE was built in 1971. Today, the country has more than a dozen top-notch courses.

Snowy Slopes

Dubai's massive Mall of the Emirates offers one of the UAE's oddest attractions—an indoor ski slope. It never snows in the UAE. But this twenty-five-story-high artificial mountain has enough room for 1,500 skiers and snowboarders!

Appealing to fans of all types, Sports City opened in Dubai in 2007. The complex includes a golf course, a tennis center, and four stadiums ranging from ten thousand to sixty thousand seats in size. The stadiums host an array of sporting events, including soccer, rugby, field hockey, and cricket matches. Sports City also houses academies that offer training in soccer, golf, and race-car driving.

The UAE has established several international competitions that attract some of the greatest athletes in the world. The top tennis players are regulars at the Dubai Tennis Championships, while top golfers come to the UAE each year for the Abu Dhabi Golf Championship and the Dubai Desert

The Dubai Tennis Championships draws many of the best players from around the world.

At the Olympics

Since 1984, the UAE has taken part in five Summer Olympics. But it was not until 2004 that an athlete from the UAE earned an Olympic medal. At that year's games, forty-year-old Sheikh Ahmad al-Maktum took the gold medal in a shooting event known as the Double Trap. A member of the ruling family of Dubai, Sheikh Ahmad was already a well-known athlete in the UAE before he took up shooting. As a young man, he was a national champion in the sport of squash.

Sheikha Maitha

Born in 1980, Sheikha Maitha bint Muhammad bin Rashid al-Maktum is the daughter of Sheikh Muhammad, the vice president of the UAE and the ruler of Dubai. She is also a star athlete, competing in the martial arts of tae kwon do and karate. In 2006, Sheikha Maitha made history at the Asian Games when she won a silver medal in karate. Her second-place showing made her the first Arab woman to win a karate medal at the competition.

Classic. The UAE has attracted attention to several events by offering record prize money. With US$6 million in prizes, the Dubai World Cup is now the richest horse race in the world. Similarly, the Dubai Marathon, starting in 2008, has the biggest purse ever offered to long-distance runners. The winner of both the men's and women's races receives US$250,000 tax free. To add a little extra drama, any winner who breaks a world record is awarded a US$1 million bonus.

Dhows and Camels

In the UAE, traditional sports lure big crowds. Dhow races in the Persian Gulf are fun events for locals and tourists alike. Some follow routes once traveled by pearl traders. The best dhow sailors know the area well and can keep their ship on course despite the shifting wind and waves.

Probably the most popular sport in the UAE is camel racing. For hundreds of years, Bedouins held contests in which skilled riders raced their fastest camels across the desert. Today, the sport is more formal. Camels are now bred like racehorses and carefully trained. Racing camels can cost as much as fine Thoroughbreds. They routinely sell for hundreds of thousands of dollars.

There are now fifteen camel racetracks in the UAE. They are often filled with tourists, many of whom have never before seen a camel. The races are similar to horse races, although betting is not allowed because Islam forbids gambling. The owners of the winning camels, however, collect prizes, which often include cars or trucks in addition to cash awards.

Camel Jockeys

In the past, camel jockeys in the UAE were generally children, some as young as five years old. Many had been kidnapped from countries in South Asia and Africa. Essentially treated as slaves, the child jockeys were forced to race. Many were injured when they lost control of their animals and fell onto the track.

Facing strong criticism from human rights groups, the UAE took action against the use of child jockeys in 2005. The government strengthened a law outlawing jockeys younger than fifteen years old or weighing less than 99 pounds (45 kilograms). It also joined with the United Nation's Children Fund (UNICEF) to launch a US$2.7 million campaign to reunite all underage camel jockeys with their parents.

Now, camel races are often run without human jockeys. The animals are instead "ridden" by small robots, which their owners operate by remote control. These robot jockeys weigh only 9 pounds (4 kg). Their light weight allows the camels to run faster, making the races more exciting than ever.

Living Day to Day

L IFE HAS CHANGED QUICKLY IN THE UAE. EVERYTHING is a mix of old and new.

Clothing is an obvious example. People walking down the streets of Dubai or Abu Dhabi wear a wide array of clothing styles. Many people wear outfits that would not look out of place in an American city. For instance, both Emirati and foreign men wear suits as they conduct business.

Opposite: **Racing camels rest at a racetrack in Abu Dhabi.**

Western suits and traditional Arab clothing are both common in the UAE.

But people wearing more traditional clothing are also common. For Emirati men, this means the *dishdasha*—a loose white garment that keeps its wearer fairly cool even in the hottest weather. For Emirati women, traditional clothing

Traditional male clothing in the UAE includes a long robe called a dishdasha and a headscarf called a *kaffiyeh*. A black cord called an *agal* holds the kaffiyeh in place.

includes the *abayya*, a black robe that covers most of the body, and a head scarf called a *shayla*. Increasingly, younger women have taken to wearing colorful, glamorous clothing under their abayyas. When a breeze shifts a robe, a passerby might spy gold jewelry or a pair of high heels on the more adventurous Emirati women.

Many Emirati women wear long, black abayyas with colorful clothes underneath.

Customers take a rest from shopping at a coffee shop in the Mall of the Emirates.

Eating in the UAE

The food eaten in the UAE shows influences from around the world. In fact, almost any cuisine can be found in restaurants there. In Dubai, anyone willing to spend what it takes can get a world-class meal made by one of the world's best chefs. Most restaurants in the country, however, are much humbler. Many cater to the foreign workers who make up most of the country's population. These often serve the everyday foods of the workers' native lands. Some of the most popular restaurants in the UAE among both foreigners and citizens serve Lebanese, Indian, or Iranian dishes.

While Emiratis enjoy foods of different nations, they also eat many traditional foods, especially at home. These include *khuzi*, roast lamb on a bed of rice, and *makbus*, a casserole made from meat or fish and rice. For sweets, Emiratis enjoy the delicious dates grown in their country and a pudding called *umm ali* that may be flavored with raisins and nuts.

Traditionally, Emiratis eat while sitting on the floor. Dishes are placed on a rug or a carpet. Generally, breakfast is light. It might just be a few dates with coffee. Lunch is the biggest meal of the day. It usually features meat or fish with rice and a few side dishes. These might include *hummus* (a dip made of ground chickpeas), *tabbouleh* (a salad made from chopped parsley, oil, and garlic), or *ful* (a salad made with fava beans.) Bread is always a part of the menu. Dinner is a smaller meal, often made from lunch's leftovers.

Bread in the UAE is typically flat. It is a staple of the Emirati diet.

Qahwah

At the beginning or end of lunch, Emiratis often enjoy a cup of *qahwah*, or coffee. They drink it unsweetened, although they often flavor it with spices, such as cardamom or cloves.

Qahwah is served in little cups that are filled just halfway. When a guest pushes the cup away and tilts it from side to side, it is a signal that the meal is over.

Family Life

Some Bedouins still live in tents as their ancestors did, but most Emiratis now live in houses or apartments. By helping pay for housing, the government has given even poor Emirates access to decent homes with electricity and running water.

Apartment buildings line the water in Dubai.

In many ways, Emirati families remain traditional. The father is often the sole breadwinner. He is regarded as the head of the household and makes most of the important family decisions. The mother is generally in charge of the house and is responsible for raising the children.

Emiratis consider children a gift from God. Parents show great love for their children, but at the same time they insist that their children follow strict rules. Children are expected to be well behaved and to show respect to their elders. In Emirati society, if a child behaves badly in public, it reflects poorly on everyone in the family.

Emirati children must attend school between the ages of six and twelve.

A Wired Nation

In recent years, the UAE has invested heavily in media and technology. As a result, its people have ready access to telephones and televisions. Nearly everyone has a phone, and almost all households have a television. Satellite dishes are widespread, so TV viewers can watch broadcasts from around the world. Computers are also common. One out of every three people in the UAE has access to the Internet.

Health Care and Education

All Emirati citizens, young and old, have benefited from the UAE government's generous funding of health care. The number of public hospitals in cities is growing, and every community of more than one thousand people has its own clinic. The government has also established traveling clinics that head into the desert to treat the nomadic Bedouins.

For citizens of the UAE, all health care is free. Foreign workers, however, must pay their own medical bills. In urban areas, a large number of private clinics and hospitals have been established to serve them.

The UAE has also made education a high priority. Before the federation was formed, few Emiratis got the chance to attend school. Now, all Emirati children are required to attend six years of primary school. Boys and girls attend separate schools.

Girls and boys go to separate schools in the UAE, but they follow the same curriculum.

Funding Marriage

The UAE government is working to promote marriage between Emirati citizens. It founded the UAE Marriage Fund in 1992 because UAE leaders were alarmed that many citizens were marrying foreigners. They feared these marriages would reduce Emiratis' interest in preserving their Arab and Muslim heritage.

Weddings in the UAE tend to be expensive. The groom must also pay money to the bride's family. To help would-be grooms, the UAE Marriage Fund now foots the bill for mass wedding ceremonies, at which as many as one hundred couples can tie the knot for free. The men below are waiting for their wedding to begin.

Older students can attend six additional years of secondary school. For the first three years, they follow a general course of study. For the following three years, students concentrate in technical, agricultural, business, or religious studies.

Recently, the UAE has adopted a plan called Education 2020 to help its students prepare for the future. The plan calls for expanding and improving science and math lessons. The Ministry of Education is also pushing for more students to learn English, since speaking English is a crucial skill for success in the business world.

For citizens of the UAE, public schools are free. The government also pays for students' meals, textbooks, and uniforms. Parents get a monthly check from the government for every child they have enrolled in school full time.

Public Holidays

New Year's Day	January 1
UAE National Day	December 2
Christmas Day	December 25

The dates of the following holidays are based upon the Islamic calendar, which is eleven days shorter than the Western calendar. Thus, their dates according to the Western calendar change from year to year.

'Id al-Adha (Feast of the Sacrifice)
Muharram (Islamic New Year)
Mawlud (Birth of Muhammad)
Accession of the Ruler of Abu Dhabi
Laylat al-Miraj (Ascension of Muhammad)
First Day of Ramadan
'Id al-Fitr (End of Ramadan)

Foreign children can attend public schools, but their parents must pay a fee. There are also private schools for noncitizens. In many, lessons are taught in English, French, German, Japanese, and other foreign languages.

Looking to the Future

Emiratis who graduate from public schools are eligible for yet another gift from the government—a free college education. Many young Emiratis take up this offer. Located in al-Ain, the United Arab Emirates University is the country's largest school of higher learning. When it opened in 1977, it had only five hundred students. Now more than fifteen thousand students attend classes there every year.

In the UAE, women are more likely than men to get an advanced degree. About 95 percent of women who complete secondary school apply for college, while just 80 percent of men do. In fact, female citizens of the UAE attend colleges and universities at a higher rate than women in any other country in the world. Women hold about 40 percent of all jobs in government and take most of the teaching positions in public schools.

The growing number of working women will undoubtedly change the shape of Emirati society. But change is hardly unknown in UAE. Since 1971, when the emirates came together, just about everything in the country has been transformed. Again and again, Emiratis have proven themselves up to the challenge of embracing new ways while preserving the best of their traditions.

Far more Emirati women than men graduate from college. Women are moving into the workforce in increasing numbers.

Timeline

United Arab Emirates History

Permanent human settlements are **ca. 3000 B.C.** established in what is now the United Arab Emirates (UAE).

People in the region domesticate camels **ca. 1000 B.C.** and develop irrigation systems.

Representatives of the Prophet **A.D. 630** Muhammad bring Islam to the region that is now the UAE.

Muhammad's successor, Caliph Abu Bakr, **632** defeats a rebel group in the Battle of Dibba in what is now al-Fujairah.

Portuguese navigator Vasco da Gama **1498** discovers a sea route between Europe and the Persian Gulf.

Portuguese and Persians battle for control **early 1500s** of the Persian Gulf.

The British compete with the Dutch for **1720s** control of Persian Gulf trade.

World History

2500 B.C. Egyptians build the pyramids and the Sphinx in Giza.

563 B.C. The Buddha is born in India.

A.D. 313 The Roman emperor Constantine legalizes Christianity.

610 The Prophet Muhammad begins preaching a new religion called Islam.

1054 The Eastern (Orthodox) and Western (Roman Catholic) Churches break apart.

1095 The Crusades begin.

1215 King John seals the Magna Carta.

1300s The Renaissance begins in Italy.

1347 The plague sweeps through Europe.

1453 Ottoman Turks capture Constantinople, conquering the Byzantine Empire.

1492 Columbus arrives in North America.

1500s Reformers break away from the Catholic Church, and Protestantism is born.

1776 The U.S. Declaration of Independence is signed.

1789 The French Revolution begins.

United Arab Emirates History

The British destroy the fleet of the Qawasim tribe and establish an army station in Ra's al-Khaimah.	1819
Sheikhs in the region that is now the UAE agree to a peace treaty with the British.	1820
The sheikhs and the British agree to the Treaty of Maritime Peace in Perpetuity; the region becomes known as the Trucial Coast.	1853
The British promise to provide the Trucial Coast with military protection in the Exclusive Agreement.	1892
The economy of the Trucial Coast is shattered as the pearl market collapses during the Great Depression.	1930s
Oil is discovered in Abu Dhabi.	1958
Oil is discovered in Dubai.	1966
The British announce their intention of withdrawing from the Trucial Coast region.	1968
The Trucial Coast sheikhdoms establish an independent nation called the United Arab Emirates.	1971
The UAE joins other nations in fighting Iraq during the Gulf War.	1991
Sheikh Zayd bin Sultan al-Nahayan, the first president of the UAE, dies; his son, Sheikh Khalifa bin Zayd al-Nahayan, becomes president.	2004

World History

1865	The American Civil War ends.
1879	The first practical light bulb is invented.
1914	World War I begins.
1917	The Bolshevik Revolution brings communism to Russia.
1929	A worldwide economic depression begins.
1939	World War II begins.
1945	World War II ends.
1957	The Vietnam War begins.
1969	Humans land on the Moon.
1975	The Vietnam War ends.
1989	The Berlin Wall is torn down as communism crumbles in Eastern Europe.
1991	The Soviet Union breaks into separate states.
2001	Terrorists attack the World Trade Center in New York City and the Pentagon in Washington, D.C.

Fast Facts

Official name: United Arab Emirates

Capital: Abu Dhabi

Official language: Arabic

Abu Dhabi

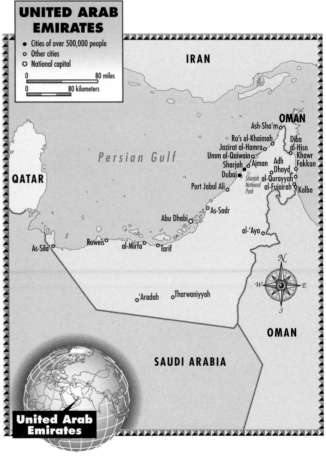

The flag of the United Arab Emirates

Desert

Official religion:	Islam
Year of founding:	1971
National anthem:	"A'ishi Biladi" ("Long Live My Country")
Government:	Federation of emirates
Chief of state:	President
Head of government:	Prime minister
Area:	32,270 square miles (83,600 square km)
Latitude and longitude of geographic center:	24° N, 54° E
Bordering countries:	Oman and Saudi Arabia
Highest elevation:	5,010 feet (1,527 m), at Jabal Yibir
Lowest elevation:	Sea level, along the coast
Hottest month:	July, average high temperature 106°F (41°C)
Coolest month:	January, average high temperature 75°F (24°C)
Highest average annual rainfall:	Sharjah Emirate, 19 inches (48 cm)
Lowest average annual rainfall:	Abu Dhabi Emirate, 3 inches (7 cm)
National population (2005):	3,769,000

Jumairah Mosque

Population of largest cities (2003):

Dubai	1,171,000
Abu Dhabi	552,000
Sharjah	519,000
Al-Ain	348,000
Ajman	225,000

Famous landmarks:

▶ *Burj al-Arab Hotel,* Dubai

▶ *The Corniche,* Abu Dhabi

▶ *Dubai Creek Golf and Yacht Club,* Dubai

▶ *Al-Fihaidi Fort,* Dubai

▶ *Al-Husn Palace,* Sharjah

▶ *Jumairah Mosque,* Dubai

Industry: Since the late 1950s, oil has been the biggest industry in the UAE. In recent years, however, the country has invested its oil income to develop other parts of the economy. By establishing tax-free trade zones, primarily in Dubai and in Abu Dhabi, the UAE has encouraged foreign companies to establish factories and offices there. The country has been particularly successful at attracting manufacturing and financial services firms. Dubai has also developed its tourism industry by building restaurants, hotels, resorts, shopping complexes, theme parks, and other attractions.

Currency: The Emirati dirham. In 2007, 3.67 dirhams equaled 1 U.S. dollar.

System of weights and measures: Metric system

Literacy rate: 78 percent

Currency

Schoolchildren

Sheikh Zayd bin Sultan al-Nahayan

Common Arabic words and phrases:

Al salaam alaykum	Hello
Ma' al-salama	Good-bye
Tisbah ala-khayr (to a man)	
Tisbihin ala-khayr (to a woman)	Good night
Fursa sa'ida.	Pleased to meet you.
Kif al-hal?	How are you?
Kif al-'a'ila?	How is your family?
Baraka Allah bik	Thank you
Afwan.	You're welcome.

Famous Emiratis:

Ahlam (Ahlam 'Ali al-Shamsi) (1969–)
Singer

Sheikh Muhammad bin Rashid
al-Maktum (1949–)
Vice president and prime minister

Sheikh Rashid bin Sa'id
al-Maktum (1912 –1990)
Prime Minister and ruler of Dubai

Sheikh Zayd bin Sultan
al-Nahayan (1918–2004)
President

Sheikha Maitha bint Muhammad
bin Rashid al-Maktum (1980–)
Tae kwon do and karate champion

Sheikh Khalifa bin Zayd
al-Nahayan (1948–)
President

Ahmad ibn Majid (ca.1432–ca.1500)
Poet and navigator

Sheikh Ahmad al-Maktum (1963–)
Olympic champion trap shooter

To Find Out More

Books

▶ Johnson, Julia. *United Arab Emirates*. Philadelphia: Chelsea House Publishers, 2000.

▶ McCoy, Lisa. *United Arab Emirates*. Philadelphia: Mason Crest Publishers, 2003.

▶ Miller, Debra A. *United Arab Emirates*. San Diego: Lucent Books, 2004.

▶ Romano, Amy. *A Historical Atlas of the United Arab Emirates*. New York: Rosen Publishing, 2004.

Web Sites

▶ **UAE at a Glance**
uaeinteract.com/uaeint_misc/glance/ataglance.pdf
A full-color brochure produced by the UAE government with up-to-the-minute information about the country.

► **UAE Interact**
www.uaeinteract.com
*Features news stories about the
UAE and includes a searchable
archive of past articles.*

► **The World Factbook:
United Arab Emirates**
https://www.cia.gov/library/
publications/the-world-factbook/
geos/ae.html
*Offers easy-to-find facts and statistics
about the UAE.*

Embassies and Organizations

► **Embassy of the United
Arab Emirates**
3522 International Court NW
Suite 400
Washington, DC 20008
202-243-2400
http://uae-embassy.org/

► **Embassy of the United Arab
Emirates in Canada**
45 O'Connor Street
Suite 1800, World Exchange Plaza
Ottawa, Ontario K1P 1A4
613-565-7272
http://www.uae-embassy.com/

Index

Page numbers in *italics* indicate illustrations.

Meet the Author

A GRADUATE OF Swarthmore College, Liz Sonneborn is a full-time writer living in Brooklyn, New York. She has written more than fifty nonfiction books for children and adults on a wide variety of subjects. Her books include *The American West, A to Z of American Indian Women, The Ancient Kushites, The Vietnamese Americans, Chronology of American Indian History*, and *Guglielmo Marconi*. She is also the author of *Yemen*, another book in the Children's Press Enchantment of the World series.

After writing *Yemen*, Sonneborn was eager to take on a book about the United Arab Emirates. "While Yemen is struggling to get a foothold in the modern era," she explains, "the UAE is now all about embracing the new. Together, the histories of the two nations tell a fascinating story about what's happening in the Middle East right now."

Finding up-to-the-minute sources of information about Yemen was difficult for Sonneborn because it is a poor nation, and its government provides little information over the Internet. But researching the UAE was a much different story.

A wealth of information about the country is available, both in print and online, especially about vibrant areas such as Dubai and Abu Dhabi. The government itself provides much information, both through news organizations it sponsors and via Web sites and online brochures designed to attract tourists and business investors to the country. Of course, any government clearly wants to cast the nation it represents in the best possible light, so the information in these sources has to be viewed critically. Nevertheless, such sources combined with outside accounts of the rapidly changing landscape of the UAE provide a picture not only of what's going on in the UAE but also of how the government and people feel about their country and its place in the world.

Photo Credits